MW00639553

NextGen
Author

How trendsetting creators use web3 and AI
to set a new standard for authorship

MALENE BENDTSEN

WEB3 changes everything

including who will win in business and publishing

#goosebump

#powertothecreators

Published by
PUBLISHING REBEL

* * *

ISBN:
978-87-972095-4-7 (paperback)
978-87-972095-5-4 (hardback)
978-87-972095-6-1 (ebook)

Learn more: https://goosebump.pub

Cover illustration: Malene Bendtsen with Craiyon (AI)
Layout: Diren Yardimli

For the authors of tomorrow...
and the people whose imagination
their books will shape

Table of Content

Introduction

We are at the edge of a new era. Web3 has entered the world of business and marketing and gained massive attention around the world. Expectations are that it is a game changer at the same scale as introducing automobiles and smartphones have been.

Web1: Read the internet
Web2: Write the internet
Web3: Own the internet

Throughout history, smart folks have quickly used new trends to get ahead of their competitors. The new world of web3 offers authors the greatest opportunity of our time to get their books to a large audience and turn readers into engaged participants.

Web3 will drive decentralisation and remove intermediaries that control assets, processes, data and decision-making. In its essence, it aims to shift power from centralised authoritative companies, institutions and governments - back to individuals. It is designed to remove every form of involvement from third parties.

Web3 will connect individuals and brands in a shared-interest way never seen before. In this new world, the masses - not authoritative intermediaries - will govern and create interest-based organisations centred around matters they care about. Now, *that* will be interesting to authors with an important message or solution to share!

Web3 provides the foundation for strategies in which readers can have a built-in interest in promoting a book for an author and allows you to set a new standard for author-reader relationships, and finally be rewarded justly in terms of the financial benefits you receive for your creative work.

> *Authors will be able to create more, sell more, and have a bigger impact - surfing the waves of technological, societal and financial trends.*

At the time of writing this book, everything is moving at the speed of light in the web3 world. What in previous giant technology leaps took a decade has happened in less than 18 months.

Pioneers have long provided and tested the technical foundation and creative business people are now building commercial solutions so the rest of us can get in and get a piece of the pie. Among the new services are author services to publish books in novel ways using NFTs.

It would be naive to think this landscape won't keep changing over the next couple of years and a 2nd edition of this book will probably be relevant within a short time. Is this book then ahead of its time? Am I too early in the market with this?

No. The change coming is big enough for me to feel obliged to shed light on the great opportunities already available to authors and publishers. You might feel it's a steep learning curve, but the good news is that you don't need to be a technical expert to use web3 to drastically increase your reach and tie your fans significantly closer to your business. And... we all need to learn about this anyway sooner or a bit later.

What I love about Web3 is that it can help solve several problems in the publishing industry and put creativity and readership back to the centre where they belong. In reality, authors are at the lowest level of the food chain and their efforts are not rewarded as they should be. Intermediaries set the rules and swallow most of the profits. It bothers me because of the unfairness and dinosaur approach to so many things in this business. But, mostly, it bothers me because independent authors are the voices shaping our imagination.

Our worldviews, culture, religions, beliefs, and so much more were for thousands of years, shaped by authors who told stories and created new unexplored worlds in the minds of readers. They presented scenarios, novel thoughts, research, theories and best practices - allowing us to learn, experience, experiment, dream and be entertained.

Books present different pseudo worlds, helping our minds in constructing imagined worlds which can translate to real worlds. They produce thoughts that shape actions and eventually create our real world. Authors set big ideas free through their writing so they can help solve important problems in the world. They deserve better than leftovers.

In a time where the next big technology revolution, web3, is happening right under our noses, creative authors can be a potent driving force in shaping the future of book publishing and, therefore, the future of distribution of big ideas and imagination.

* * *

This book is a trailblazer showing the best and most applicable way to get into the game before the masses arrive so you benefit from the PR opportunities related to this very hot trending topic.

I'll be sharing with you multiple ways to incorporate web3 quickly, effectively and with little or no technical expertise. These will help you:

a. Use your book to position yourself as a known authority at the forefront of your industry;
b. Build an audience around the world as keen to spread your idea or message as you are;
c. Reward readers in new ways so they become loyal customers and active co-promoters;
d. Create multiple innovative products out of a single book manuscript;
e. .... And much more!

Doing business in web3 is still an untested territory. You will see that the train has not only left the platform but is ploughing its way through the landscape of business at an increasingly high speed.

To follow what happens in business, marketing and publishing and be inspired by what other authors do, visit Goosebump.pub or follow on social media.

Happy reading!

MALENE BENDTSEN
Publishing rebel and knowledge liberator

How to read this book

Part 1: The Disruption
This part address the societal, economic and technical trends that are the forces behind the changes we see in the book industry. It's essential to understand the actual game changer in web3 and become familiar with the associated language. We also look at the reasons why the publishing industry is likely to be massively impacted by this game changer.

Part 2: The Power of NFTs
The most useful part of web3 for authors is the NFTs. After explaining what NFTs are and the different motivations people have for buying them, we dive deeper into what they can do. I also present two use cases to spark your imagination about how you might use them.

Part 3: Authorship reimagined
Our perception of what a book is and how it is created is quite ancient. We look into how to creatively and efficiently use novel book formats that will stand out in the market. You'll also learn how NFTs can change how you build a high-quality audience, invested in your book, mission, project or business.

Part 4: Start the NFT engine
We bring it back to making strategic and tactical decisions about your authorship, business, and book. I give you a framework to decide the best and most potent way forward, depending on your business goals and characteristics of your audience.

PART 1
The
Disruption

The internet hasn't really happened yet.

- HISTORIAN **JOSH ROSENTAHL**

CHAPTER 1
Power to the people

The sudden escalation of the use of web3 *technologies* in business is rooted in a *societal* trend; Power to the people. And they become especially relevant to you as an author because of the *economic* trends in publishing. Chapters 1-3 shed light on how these forces combined have the potential to change *everything* in the book industry - and beyond.

Web3 intends to build a new world order in which power is distributed among large groups of individuals as opposed to power being concentrated around very few people.

Web3 enthusiasts today aim at what pioneers intended it to be from the very beginning; a transparent, co-governed, co-owned, co-empowered and co-created world in which no authorities can suppress, exploit, or dictate the rules. A people-to-people system that is fully owned by the people.

We are quite used to thinking technology changes our worldviews, imagination, behaviours and values. But in reality, Web3 is only the enabling technology of a much bigger social phenomenon that has influenced all of us for decades and that has now found its way to publishing and many other industries. So before I explain how the technology works and how you can use it, it's important that we first visit the significant societal (and economic) change it seeks to implement.

* * *

On February 15, 1971, Billy Preston, Bobby Keys, Jim Gordon, Klaus Voormann, and Rosetta Hightower stepped into Ascot Sound Studios at Tittenhurst Park on the outskirts of London to produce what would become the *Imagine* album.

That John Lennon was concerned with world peace, equality and human rights comes as no surprise. During sessions, they would record 'quickies', explained by Lennon as 'songs for people to sing'. On this day (February 15, 1971), the day I was born, 'Power to the People' was recorded.

Lennon wasn't the first person to use this phrase though. The Black Panther Party (BPP) used it on a poster in March 1969, and jazz saxophonist Joe Henderson picked up on the slogan and recorded an album with the title 'Power to the People' in May 1969.

The Black Panther Party's poster 'Berkely Liberation Program' encouraged a revolution at Berkeley University:

   a. *Destroy the university unless it serves the people*
   b. *Break the power of landlords, housing for everyone*
   c. *Tax corporations, not the working people*
   d. *Create people's government*
   e. *Power to the imagination*[1]

History includes other significant events regarding this subject, like the Emancipation Proclamation in 1863, women's right to vote (for most of the western countries between 1915-1925), or the end of apartheid in the 1990s. These important events are recognised as milestones on the journey towards a better world.

The revolution against authorities, which began in the 60s and 70s, has taken up less space in the minds of most people in democratic countries in the past 30 years. We have articulated our concerns and perhaps taken action to create change, mostly from a human rights perspective.

* * *

Most people will agree that important decisions shaping our everyday reality have been - and are still - the business of privileged white, often middle-aged men. But few realise how *few* they are, even at a global level. Huge corporations, governments, social media, banks, and more - are run by a small group of powerful people who can set the rules.

That is not necessarily a problem. Not to most of us who are indeed living privileged lives ourselves. But in the last decade people have realised that what at an individual or local level might feel like a privileged life has a larger price tag to it.

The world has so many significant problems, that we have lost our faith they will ever be resolved at a political level. Some have to do with climate change, human rights suppression, and world peace. Others feel closer to home like financial instability, meaningless jobs producing meaningless products, greedy banks, companies taking advantage and controlling our personal data, or unevenly distributed access to education.

Given these problems result from the decision made or not made, it fertilised the ground with a stronger and stronger request for change in how decisions are made. The system doesn't work and the price is too high.

To make a long story short, trust in authorities to act in the best (short and long-term) interest of common people is decreasing and, most times, gone. People are seeking to take back the power. Only, it's hard to see how it's possible to change within the current system.

* * *

While many of us only recently began to do our part and changed our daily behaviours, i.e. to protect the planet from overheating, a group of pioneers was for decades working together on building the technological backbone for a new world order, which all weaknesses and shortcomings aside, will change both your world and mine. Much is uncertain still, but there is little doubt that blockchain technology (web3) will create radical change.

Not going into all the technical details, a brief look into the history of how this backbone was developed provides insights into the intent behind the blockchain technology; Decentralisation of power.

Instead of building systems to manage trust, these pioneers intended to create systems in which trust in human behaviour became obsolete. Once a creator (you or me) defines how a transaction shall be carried out, all transactions are carried out the same way. No nepotism, racism, corruption, tampering with data, or individual opinions. And all 100% transparent in public records.

Most times, people's understanding of what blockchains are is limited to cryptocurrency, often perceived to be unreal or even fake money and a 'dodgy game for speculators'. You'll see it started with crypto (very real digital cash) but doesn't end there.

Below, I summarise how it played out:

- Referred to as "the father of online anonymity", and "the godfather of cryptocurrency", David Chaum[2] is recognized as the inventor of digital cash. He first proposed a blockchain-like protocol in his 1982 dissertation "Computer Systems Established, Maintained, and Trusted by Mutually Suspicious Groups. His work also includes trustworthy voting systems and anonymous communication protocols.

- Stuart Haber and W. Scott Stornetta described a secured chain of blocks in 1991 in which document timestamps could not be tampered with.

- Satoshi Nakamoto improved the design so blocks were timestamped without requiring them to be signed by a trusted party in 2008. The design became a core component of the cryptocurrency Bitcoin, where it serves as the public ledger (irreversible recording) for all transactions on the network.

By reaching a 13.5% adoption rate within financial services in 2016, blockchain technology reached the early adopters' phase.[34]

The same year, industry trade groups joined to create the Global Blockchain Forum, an initiative of the Chamber of Digital Commerce.

An article from Forbes[5] states that The International Data Corp has estimated that corporate investment in blockchain technology will reach $12.4 billion by 2022. The article is worth a study covering almost any imaginable industry, from finance and tuna fishing to brewing and a global blockchain for shippers, TradeLens, led by Danish Maersk. Blockchain pioneers and investors have put their time and money where their mouth is.

* * *

Blockchain technology has until recently - by laymen - very much been related to the worlds of gaming and financial speculation. It was until a few years easy to conclude that Crypto land is a playing field for tech geeks and get-rich-quick dreamers. But it's important to understand that a more profound desire for *societal change* has been the driving force all along and still is.

Disrupting technology has river-like behaviour. The water will follow the path of less resistance and, in the end, flood everything. Decentralised finance (DEFI) and the revolutionary change in banking business are, however, just a stepping stone into a much larger shift in technology that will disrupt many industries, change our behaviours and redistribute power.

In fact, I suggest that despite the importance of cryptocurrency, these new currencies are the least interesting part of this revolutionising technology. Perhaps the American people's (a group of crypto investors) attempt to buy the Constitution in November 2021[6] nails my point and shows you how strong this force is.

A guy posted a simple Tweet with zero expectation of a response, suggesting that people came together to buy the last known privately held copies of the constitution (out of 13 remaining copies in total) that were coming up for auction at Sotheby's. From there, a series of almost unimaginable events took place.

In a five-day stretch, Constitution DAO (a specific new type of organisation that we will come back to later) was created with the intent to collect enough money to win the auction and purchase the Constitution[7].

Around $47 million[8] was donated through a social media campaign. The average contribution was $206,26[9] and around 17,437 people donated, bearing witness to the fact that people cared. My guess is they didn't care about owning a piece of the book. They cared about the message.

To the disappointment of the contributors, the DAO offer was too low to win the auction. Determining what to do with the money and how to continue the DAO was messy. In the end, they offered backers their money back as stated in the initial contract ('burn' the token) or to keep their token and do whatever they wanted with it.[1011]

In the following months, backers could sell their $PEO-PLE tokens (coming back to tokens too) in secondary markets (think eBay) at an elevated price. It went down pretty quickly though and at the time of finishing this script, we have yet to see how many will claim their money back and how many will start new initiatives using $PEOPLE tokens.

* * *

So what have we learned here? Hopefully, you get a sense of how the change happening has been building up over decades. The development of blockchain technology that enables web3 started 40 years ago, even if we only started seeing applications of it in recent years.

We are not talking about immature, unfinished experiments but a full-fledged new internet with a new set of rules. A game changer equal to social media or the computer itself. And it's all designed to create a more effective, more stable and more honest system - for the people, owned and governed by the people.

Had Lennon lived today, he might have added another verse to *Imagine*, right after "imagine no possessions"...

> *Imagine no authorities*
> *No single person too small*
> *No crazy rules to obey*
> *A powerhood of all*
>
> *Imagine all the people*
> *Sharing all the world*
>
> *You may say I'm a dreamer*
> *But I'm not the only one*
> *I hope someday you'll join us*
> *And the world will live as one*

CHAPTER 2

Publishing: A candidate for disruption

Who makes money in publishing

What makes me believe book publishing is one of the first industries to experience the impact of web3 is that the industry presents all the significant indicators making an industry a disruption candidate, including but not only financial indicators.

In lay terms, it's not a 'happy' and well-functioning industry. *Dissatisfaction* has characterised book publishing over a long period. Dissatisfaction with profits across many entities, dissatisfaction with how data is treated, and dissatisfaction with who controls the few systems everybody depends on. Let's break it down to see how the industry works.

Book publishing revenue worldwide amounts to $122 billion USD[12]. The net revenue of the US book publishing industry has sat at a level of 25.63-27.96 billion USD since 2008, decreasing in recent years[13].

So the first interesting observation is that publishing is not growing even though the number of adults who reads has increased. The 30-64 age group experienced the biggest increase but also readers among young people increased. No age group declined. The 65+ age group plateaued.

Another interesting observation is that the publishing industry is consolidating, meaning big players are becoming bigger and stronger[14]. In the US, Penguin Random House, Macmillan, Hachette Book Group, and HarperCollins are the dominant players, accounting for around 80% of industry revenue[15].

	Imprints (publisher brands)	Titles per year
Penguin Random House	275	70,000
Hachette Book Group	150	16,000
HarperCollins	120	10,000
Simon and Schuster	35	2,000[16]
Macmillan	32[17]	Not found

The 'big 5' publishers[18] may become the 'big 4' unless a merger between Penguin Random House and Simon and Schuster is blocked as a result of an antitrust investigation (ongoing at the time of writing)[19]. The very presence of an antitrust investigation is a testament to the extreme power held by very few players.

Anyway, these publishers posted impressive gains in earnings in 2021 over 2020[20], which must mean that - since there was no growth in the industry - smaller publishers are earning less.

In the first 15 years of this century, the number of privately held publishing establishments in the US was stable at around 34,500-36,500. However, this number was by 2021 more than doubled[21], most likely representing the increased number of self-publishing indie authors.

The same is happening among bookstores with a few dominating retailers and smaller book shops struggling to survive. Amazon accounts for 55% of book sales[22].

The small-publisher field is blurry with indie authors, hybrid publishers and traditional publishing houses. For the point, I am trying to make, diving into details doesn't matter though.

What is crystal clear is that fewer and bigger publishers are gaining a bigger part of profits, leaving the remaining profits to be shared among the increased number of smaller publishers. The question is if that is a problem or not and for who.

What makes an industry open to disruption

All industries undergo a four-phase life cycle; introduction, growth, maturity and decline[23]. The publishing industry is far from introduction and growth and at least well into the maturity stage with zero growth as stated in the previous section.

But there is an important point to make here. More people are reading more books. As we have seen, the 'reading'-market (including audio) is not declining. But publishing as a traditional industry has not managed to take part in the growth that's there if we define it as a 'reading'-market.

The official numbers of the publishing industry do not include self-published books. I didn't come across any information on whether they include print-on-demand or not. But I am sure they do not include books printed and sold by individual authors directly to readers or companies. This part of the market is ignored to an extent where popular bestseller lists don't acknowledge even bestselling authors who sold far more books because their books are self-published.

What does all of this mean? It means that if the total reading market is growing, and traditional publishers are not, then their market share is, in fact, declining.

Why should you care about this as an author? Because new technologies will eventually disrupt declining industries and often with a different business model as the result. This means new opportunities for those who are quick to take advantage. And this is especially true if there is also dissatisfaction with how the industry works.

The decline phase marks the end of an industry's ability to support growth. So you might wonder how the biggest publishers continue to grow and swallow up bit by bit of the market.

As we have seen with the Penguin-Simon and Schuster merge, further consolidation is common. The biggest publishers can most likely continue to grow through mergers, adding revenue to the topline and reducing costs through internal synergies and cost reductions.

We see the same thing happening in many sectors i.e. the financial sector or retail. The smaller boats (smaller banks, insurance companies, publishers, grocery stores) disappear into the stomach of the giant whales, Moby Dick style.

As defined by Investopedia, decline often signals 'the end of viability for the incumbent business model', pushing industry participants into adjacent (next) markets. In plain English, this means everything will change.

They can delay the decline phase with large-scale product improvements or repurposing, but such improvements merely tend to prolong the process[24]. Publishers will have to reinvent their service to a degree that they *become* the adjacent market (which we will soon explore).

Now, the interesting question is how likely it is that they can and will reinvent their service, or if they will continue to seek growth in a business-as-usual fashion, finding more other publishers to buy to get a bigger market share and show enough growth to the shareholders who expect them to grow.

The three determining factors of a company's ability to innovate are; if it had significant previous success, the company size and, how old the company is. We already know that the biggest four hold 80% of the US market[25] so check-check on both previous success and company size. But how about age?

Six of the world's top ten publishers are from before 1920, four of which go back to before 1850. The remaining four were established within the past 30 years but in most parts on the backbone of existing and very mature media companies.

The age factor is relevant because old industries and companies have developed a 'fixed' mindset (on top of complex technical infrastructure). Certain beliefs about what will work are hard to change - because they so far worked! This exact mindset, these specific educational backgrounds that they rely on, these processes, these values…. They worked and have built the company's success in the past!

I have the deepest respect for the high levels of skills and competence and the fact that the people in these industries managed to grow the business to the level it's at right now. Unfortunately, that confidence in what works and many years of avoiding risk and delivering predictable results is also the strongest enemy of innovation.

Zero of the top 10 companies were born into a digital age and - to the best of my knowledge - they are all focused on mass market expansion in a paper-first business model. Their vast experience in doing what they do, keeping their noses to the grindstone, causes the peripheral vision to diminish.

Even if someone presents a bright idea, it will likely not survive until implementation. A great example of this is when Kodak invented the first-ever digital camera in 1975. Instead of using their invention to elevate and redefine the business, they killed it to protect their primary source of income, film rolls. Kodak filed for bankruptcy in 2012 after the digital camera patent expired in 2007.

I have first-hand experience as a former head of innovation in one of Scandinavia's biggest insurance companies and I can tell you that even if there is *will* it is not easy to move faster, especially in a new direction.

It is difficult to protect today's revenue sources while building revenue streams for tomorrow. In the company I worked for, there were 800 IT systems, a gazillion different ways of defining a customer and an insane amount of technical leftovers from decades of mergers.

Few companies with more than a century of age are agile. They are turtles and move slowly, opening up the playfield for more innovative newcomers who will put customer value and experience at the centre of their attention and deliver a higher level of satisfaction and excitement to either customers or suppliers, or both.

The fuel that will light the fire

Authors get, on average, 10% royalty with traditional publishing. It amazes me how long a **sense of unfair profit distribution** has prevailed in the industry without significant change happening. Self-publishing has been the answer to the difficulties of being accepted by a traditional publisher. But has it also solved the profitability problem?

For self-publishers, earnings can be higher or lower than when traditionally published. It depends on how it's created, printed, published, and distributed. The most profitable way of self-publishing would be to use the same system traditional publishers use, printing books yourself.

In this scenario, you are a traditional publisher, but an independent one that calls your own shots and doesn't share your profit with an external publishing house. If you are selling your books directly to consumers or companies via your website and email list, you will earn maximum profit, only subtracting printing costs, shipping and handling costs from book sales.

It is however also riskier (i.e. estimating book sales correctly) and it requires an initial investment in printing. In terms of marketing, it often comes as a surprise to authors that they are, in fact, largely expected to sell their books themselves whether or not they have a publisher.

Self-publishing in the traditional model is not a new thing. That was always possible. Print-on-Demand (PoD) was the innovation that changed *how* many authors choose to self-publish. You upload a print-ready file that fits the technical requirements to a PoD platform. Then, that platform will make it available to all bookstores through a centralised system (which is the same system used for traditionally published books).

Online bookstores have no reason not to include your book in their catalogue and their systems will create a page for your book based on the information you provided when uploading your book.

Physical bookstores have limited shelf space and are more selective. They also require a return policy which doesn't always go hand-in-hand with the policies of the self-publishing platform you use (far from).

In terms of profits, your earnings depend on the book format, the number of pages and how many pages are to be printed in colour. A high-quality, coloured, 250 pages book published using a PoD solution will have quite low-profit margins.

I am not saying this to discourage you, but to let you know you need to be smart about your book design and learn how to navigate this minefield. There are better profits to be made if you do it right.

Apart from the sense of unfairness in terms of who makes money from the hard and creative work of the author, there are other unfortunate traits that add fuel to potential disruption.

Authors receive **zero customer data** and have no direct way to take the conversation beyond the book or use customer data strategically in their marketing. They can - and should - create additional bonuses and provide a reason for people to look them up on their websites, and they should create sales funnels to sell other products and services to those who choose to give their email address or otherwise get in touch with the author. But many authors don't get any of the customer data, even though the online bookstores know who they are (I couldn't find a percentage of how many books are sold online but it's safe to say by far the most of print and all digital).

Books as a product have stalled. Sufficient data is not available, but each year somewhere between two and four million book titles are published[26]. And even though the paper format is still preferred with 40% of retail revenue being hardcover book sales, 20% (and rising) of consumers listen to audiobooks and the penetration of ebooks is 15%.

The digital formats hold the potential to create a different reading experience. Yet, because profits rely on print volume keeping development costs to a minimum, all readers get the same experience, in a 'one size fits all'-approach to product development.

Authors and publishers are rarely taking advantage of multimedia opportunities, i.e. adding video to an ebook. Instead, the manuscript is turned into four formats with the same content and little adaption to the specific format, or to segmented target groups.

The underlying force creating this is a cemented belief that volume is the sole denominator of profitability (which it was in a print-only, non-digital world). This is also why the first-edition or limited-edition concepts are no longer used as a higher-gain strategy. Low volume makes little sense in a print-only regime. But it very much does in web3!

Copyright infringement is another well-known problem in book publishing, and might in reality be one of the primary reasons to choose a traditional publisher. They geared their organisations towards protecting your creative work. The only problem is that you will have to sign over copyrights to your publisher to access that protection.

Copyright infringement can happen in (at least) two ways. We obtain copyrights in the moments of creation. However, it is not always easy to prove who was the original creator - or to credit the original creator of a concept, model or idea that you as an author want to include in your work. A recent example among my own authors was an author who wanted to give credit for the use of the Japanese Ikigai model. It was extremely complicated to identify the source.

Copyright infringement can happen deliberately or unintentionally as already existing content inspires the author. As a short-term solution, I suggest you use one of the multiple available tools to check your work for plagiarism so that you are not infringing on anyone's rights.

There is very little you can do to prevent someone from printing copies of your books and selling them as originals. Regarding ebooks, Amazon will deliver your ebook to an e-reader and the buyer will not get the actual file. Other bookstores will email the file to the buyer, pointing out it's for personal use only and that it is not legal to share the content. Or they will add DRM protection which is a bit of a pain in the arse to readers.

I guess we all lent a friend a book from time to time. Perhaps we are, in that case, copying the experience and learning without compensating the creator. The only difference to copying the book is that the person sharing it has no personal gain from doing so.

I would argue that the problem might not be a lack of compensation if the purpose is to build a loyal and engaged fanbase. It might, in fact, be in the author's interest that the book has as much reach as possible which is also why many authors - especially nonfiction authors - give books away for free.

Most authors do not get their principal source of income from book sales directly but from related activities. The simple solution to the perception that this (people getting access to our books without us being compensated) is a problem is a matter of perspective - and whether there is truth in it depends on the author's business model. But both pirating and lack of crediting are genuine problems authors and publishers deal with.

Overproduction of books is another problem in the industry, less spoken of. Many unsold books are destroyed every year worldwide. In order to keep printing costs per book down, we keep the printing volumes up, producing larger editions.

I wonder if, across a giant publisher's production, it's more profitable to keep those volumes up, or if what is saved in print cost per book is lost in storage costs and waste.

Does it make sense to prioritise the discipline of exact market demand estimation with the purpose of maximising profit over a strategic intent to change market behaviour towards digital no-paper and therefore no-waste formats (perhaps by making these formats a more interesting experience)? I love the paper format but overproduction is a serious problem across many industries, including publishing.

To wrap things up, there are several indicators that the book publishing industry can improve. In the next chapter, we will look into why web3 is relevant in this context, but I want to ensure, you learn about this with a solid understanding of some problems the industry (and authors in particular) faces.

Explained with the innovation concept developed by authors W. Chan Kim and Renée Mauborgne[27]; publishing is a red ocean. Too many sharks fighting over too little food in bloody waters.

I doom publishing to be reinvented for several reasons (I've added a few more not even mentioned above):

a. Consolidation: Very mature, big-sized market leaders capturing 80% of market revenue
b. Strong perception of unfair distribution of profits
c. Author-reader gap with all customer data out of reach for authors
d. Under-utilisation of the capabilities of digital formats
e. Overproduction of books
f. Niche books that need financing
g. Few minds create for the masses
h. … and: Technology that holds the potential to offer brand new business models

CHAPTER 3
The game changer

Web3 and blockchain technology

After exploring the societal trend 'Power to the People' and the economical trend 'Publishing as a candidate for disruption', we move on to understand the technology and how it is a game changer.

Web3 is a collaborative, anti-authoritarian open source technology, brand and community-managed world. Where very few people have the power to set the rules of the game in web2, there are pretty much no rules, no company structure and nobody who holds authority solitary in web3. It's libertarian and very much 'Power to the People'. Thousands of people are developers of the blockchain but nobody owns it. Apart from being a radical technological innovation, it is also nothing less than a business model revolution with an enormous impact on who is in power happening right under our noses.

Web3 is in the very early adoption phase, meaning pioneers have been building the infrastructure to a level where big brands see how to use it to take their communities to the next level - and sometimes even make enthusiasts co-owners. A bit later in the book, you'll find some use cases but examples from many industries are mushrooming every day.

* * *

Simplified, Web3 is an umbrella term for blockchain, NFTs, metaverse, crypto etc. It's the new internet which people like you and me *own*. We are no longer just readers of content or contributors of content. We own it because we either bought it or created it.

Everything you'll hear about in this book is built on blockchain technology. That is the underlying infrastructure that enables NFTs, metaverse, crypto etc. IBM defines[28] blockchain as "a shared, immutable ledger that facilitates the process of recording transactions and tracking assets in a business network." An asset can be tangible (a house, car, cash, land) or intangible (intellectual property, patents, copyrights, branding). In its simplest form, a blockchain is a database.

However, there is so much more to this revolutionary technology than that. Blockchain technology can revolutionise everything from how we do business, how we document important information like ownership, or who earned how much on certain assets - even how we interact with one another.

As mentioned in chapter 1, blockchain technology was first proposed by a person or group of people known as Satoshi Nakamoto in 2008. However, the true identity of Satoshi Nakamoto remains a mystery to this day. We know that Satoshi Nakamoto's vision for blockchain technology was to create a decentralised system that would allow for peer-to-peer transactions with no need for a third party, such as a bank. Therefore blockchain technology is often referred to as "the internet of value". It has the potential to transform the way we interact with and transfer value within our society.

One of the key ways blockchain technology is expected to transform how we interact with and transfer value within our society is through application of smart contracts. Smart contracts are self-executing contracts that are stored on a blockchain (technically they are a piece of programming). Everything stored on the blockchain implies transactions are public and immune to fraud or manipulation.

Smart contracts can be used for various purposes, such as contract negotiations, insurance claims, real estate transactions, or even book royalties. They have the potential to streamline processes and make them more efficient and cost-effective, with transactions being completed within minutes. Imagine receiving your book royalties in real time! In chapter 4, we will dive a lot deeper into the functionality of smart contracts. For now, just think of them as digital contracts, programmed to run sequences of code to complete if-then actions quickly. When this event happens, do this. For example, when this book is sold, pay the author x%. Or your mother-in-law. That's up to you.

* * *

Another way that blockchain technology is expected to transform the way we interact with and transfer value within our society is through the use of digital currencies. Digital currencies are cryptocurrencies that are stored on a blockchain. Some people believe that cryptocurrencies, such as Bitcoin, are not real money because they are not backed by a government or a central bank. However, others believe cryptocurrencies are real money because they can be used to make regular purchases - some of them even in the physical world.

The crypto economy is booming, and it is a matter of fact that the economy is too significant to ignore. There are now over 10,000 active cryptocurrencies and around 300 million cryptocurrency users across the globe. And 18,000 businesses now accept crypto as payment[29]. Cryptocurrencies are becoming more and more mainstream as more people use them to purchase digital and physical goods and services.

Clearly, the crypto economy is not going away anytime soon. So, what does this mean for businesses? It means that businesses need to take cryptocurrencies seriously and begin accepting them as payment methods and make it just as easy and compelling as paying with a credit card, PayPal or similar.

There are several benefits for businesses that accept cryptocurrencies as payment methods. Cryptocurrencies are global currencies. You can conduct transactions with anyone in the world, regardless of their location - and it won't cost you any more than transferring money to your neighbour. The transaction fees (called gas fees) are much lower than the fees associated with traditional payment methods such as credit cards, not to mention international money transfer fees which average 12%[30].

Second, cryptocurrencies are digital currencies, which means that they are instant and secure. The efficiency of the blockchain ensures that your auntie 2,000 miles away will safely receive the digital cash within minutes.

Third, cryptocurrencies have the potential to become a lever for low-income populations in regions that struggle with fraud, corruption and lack of financial security and help them become an integral part of a global economy. In the same way, blockchain could help improve documentation of land or real estate ownership in countries where not even a shitload of bureaucracy ensures property rights are respected.

If you have trouble imagining this is a problem, I can tell you people lose their houses every day, not because they didn't pay but because somebody tampered with the paperwork. While living in Peru, I bared witness to a friend's aunt having her house stolen while she was on a weekend getaway. Papers changed, locks changed. This happened in Lima, a city with a population of 10 million. Imagine what is happening in more rural areas around the globe.

* * *

One of the most well-known digital currencies is Bitcoin. Bitcoin was the first digital currency to be successfully implemented.

Since its launch, Bitcoin has experienced significant growth and has become widely accepted as payment:

a.   Over 15,000 businesses worldwide accept Bitcoin, 2,300 in the US (June, 2022)
b.   There are 36,659 Bitcoin ATMs in the U.S.[31]

Ethereum is another popular digital currency. It was launched in 2015 and has experienced significant growth in popularity. Just like Bitcoin, Ethereum can pay for goods and services online. In addition, Ethereum can also pay for goods and services offline. 28% of American small businesses accepted cryptocurrency as payment in 2020[32].

As mentioned, there are many other cryptocurrencies. What's important here is that they are built on different blockchains that support different purposes. A coin is created on its own blockchain and Bitcoin, for example, was created to be used as a digital currency. The Ethereum blockchain was created primarily as a platform for smart contracts and is used to execute contracts between parties, even though it also has its own coin, Ether (ETH).

How do blockchain transactions happen?

To understand how blockchain technology works, it is first important to understand what a block is. A block is a digital record of a transaction. These transactions can be anything from financial transactions to simple messages or even voting records. Transactions are, in their essence, 'something' sent from 'someone' to 'someone else'.

One of the most important aspects of blockchain technology is that it is decentralised. This means that no central authority, such as a bank, controls the network. Instead, the network is controlled by all of the users who are part of it. This makes it secure and resilient to attacks.

Once a transaction is started, a new block is created.

When the block has been created, it is added to the chain of existing blocks, hence the term "blockchain". Each block in the chain is connected to the other blocks through what blockchain nerds call a cryptographic hash function (you and I can call it a mathematical algorithm). This ensures that each block is securely linked to the one before it and after it in the chain.

New blocks are created through a process known as mining. In order to mine a new block, computers on the network must solve a complex mathematical problem. Anyone who owns a computer can become a miner. However, to be successful (it's a business), you need specialised hardware and software. In addition, you also need to be part of a mining pool, which is a group of miners who work together to mine new blocks.

Anyways... I don't suppose you are here to become a miner, so moving on...

The first computer (miner) to solve the problem is rewarded with a certain number of "tokens". These tokens can be used to purchase goods and services or even traded for other currencies. This built-in mechanism will incentivise mining to happen as quickly as possible. Therefore many processes are executed much faster in web3.

The technology is secure because each block in the chain is linked to the one before it and after it through the cryptographic hash function (the complex math again). In order to change a single block, you would need to change every block that comes after it in the chain. This makes it nearly impossible to tamper with data stored on a blockchain.

On top of that blockchain-based transactions are transparent. This means that all participants in the network can see every transaction that takes place. This help to build trust and confidence in the system. These two factors arc the reasons blockchain enthusiasts call it a trustless system - there is no need to trust any humans.

* * *

The biggest challenges blockchain technology is facing are scalability and energy consumption. Each block in the chain needs to be verified by all of the computers on the network before it can be added. As the number of transactions increases, it becomes more and more difficult to add new blocks in a timely manner. And mining new blocks requires a lot of computing power if verification is required by all computers in the network. This can lead to high electricity costs and environmental damage.

Newer blockchains use a technique called "sharding" to split up the blockchain into smaller parts. This allows the network to process more transactions at a faster rate. While first-generation blockchains use a method called 'proof of work', second-generation blockchains use a technique called "proof of stake" to reduce the amount of energy required for mining. Proof of stake allows nodes (computers that take part in a blockchain network) to verify transactions without needing to solve a complex mathematical problem. This reduces the amount of energy needed and makes the process much more efficient.

Third-generation blockchains are designed to solve the scalability and energy consumption issues faced by first and second-generation blockchains. Newer blockchains process more transactions faster and with less energy required.

During the weeks I am finishing this book, Ethereum announced plans to rid itself of the energy-intensive code, and cut 99% of its energy[33].

* * *

Phew… that was a lot of new and perhaps a little complex information. For publishers and authors, there are five core elements of web3 you should know *enough* about to consider how web3 might help you reach readers, sell more books and build your business or author career:

1. **Cryptocurrencies (which we already covered)**
   Your audience will soon expect to use cryptocurrencies as a payment option

2. **The Metaverse (covered in this chapter)**
   Your audience will soon have a virtual identity and expect in time also to find you in their virtual world.

3. **DAOs (covered in this chapter)**
   People will to a much higher degree take part (and invest in) organisations centred around things that matter to them.

4. **Social tokens (covered in this chapter)**
   Your own coins within your community. They can also be used to reward specific behaviour but also for crowdfunding.

5. **NFTs (covered in depth in chapter Part II)**
   In my opinion, NFTs are the most interesting part of web3 for authors at this point. For this reason, we go much deeper into them.

Even though not all 5 are equally potent or easy to successfully implement at this point (or equally relevant to all audience sizes or types of businesses, I dedicated enough space to them so you can educate yourself enough to consider your long-term vision before making any short-term move.

There is zero doubt in my mind that 1) and 2) are inevitable at some point, and I find 3) DAOs super compelling and it is something that I will continue to learn about. Social tokens might be relevant, but NFTs are something you can work with TODAY. You can get this book as an NFT: goosebump.pub/nextgen-author-book.

And now to a brief introduction to the Metaverse, DAOs and social tokens.

What is the Metaverse?

The metaverse is a term used to describe the digital world that exists alongside our physical world. It was first coined in 1992 and sci-fi movies have helped us imagine what it could look like. It's a place where people can interact with each other and with digital items in a realistic way.

Imagine a world where you can meet up with your friends, play games, host a global book reading, do a TED talk or shop in digital stores - from anywhere you are, no travelling required. Or imagine you can't go to your favourite event of the year. To me, that's Social Media Marketing World in San Diego (SMMW). Instead, you can enter the Metaverse, find the event, go to the session you'd like to be a part of, and find a seat right next to your friend from last year's event. You might even choose to show up as your digital avatar, your second identity.

It sounds very futuristic. But some of the biggest companies in the world are already creating amazing experiences in the Metaverse. For example, Coca-Cola reimagined its popular 1956 vending machine, the Happiness Machine[34], for a virtual reality version. And Nissan[35] has created a virtual test drive experience that lets people try out its cars. Even Fashion Week was hosted in the Metaverse this year[36] (as well as in the physical world).

Publishers and authors can use the metaverse to connect with new readers and promote their books to them. The metaverse provides a new way to interact with audiences that traditional publishing methods don't reach.

For example, you could host virtual book signings or create interactive reading experiences. Readers can meet the author and other fans, and discuss the book in a realistic setting. This is a great way to get people engaged with the book and to promote discussion.

You could also create virtual previews of books. This is a great way to give readers a taste of the book and hook them into reading it. Or to create educational experiences that let students explore different topics in a fun and interactive way. The possibilities are endless!

* * *

It is important to note that the Metaverse is not here yet, even if that's the term widely used. There are multiple virtual spaces where you can create events. Eventually, they will become one gigantic system with many 'local' spaces like in the physical world.

You will have a digital identity that might differ from your identity in the physical world. You will dress your avatar, join different virtual spaces and build your digital network. It will be *one* virtual representation of you - across platforms, not a new avatar you create on each new platform you want to join. You'll be able to purchase different items such as clothes, houses, cars, etc. You can even run a business or join a concert in India along with your friend who is in Australia.

Sounds like something far into the future? Something 'you'd never'? Well, the behaviour is already there among younger generations, even if you don't understand it yet. For gamers, this is just a logical next step. They have been pioneering and trained to navigate a world many of us are having a hard time coming to terms with. But here is a big hint you *will* eventually be part of this: Facebook changed its company name to Meta and invested 10 billion USD in 2021 to develop a metaverse[37] (Facebook is not *the* metaverse, even if they'd like you to assume it's their creation, calling themselves Meta).

One side of the story is that Facebook is - like any other centralised organisation controlling our data, transactions and online experience - at risk of being taken over by web3 at some point if they don't bridge the current business model to a blockchain-empowered one (so of cause they will).

This bridging the physical world with the metaverse, includes crypto payments and payouts, and integrate token features into their existing platforms. Both the Facebook brand and the Instagram brand are already working on this, as are many online merchants.

Another side of the story is that the way technology works today has some significant limitations on what kind of experience Facebook and others can build. The core of the experience today is the specific app that you are using, and it is very hard (or impossible) to integrate your data, possessions, access or what you do on one platform to the next.

However, in web3 everything is centred around *you* and you can seamlessly move items you own between different platforms and into virtual spaces. Also, it will be you *owning* a part of the internet, not just using it.

As 5G broadbands are rolled out, the power to roll out internet in 3D is in place and this is one of the reasons the development of the metaverse is escalating now.

What are DAOs

DAOs are Decentralised Autonomous Organisations. They are organisations that exist on the blockchain and are run by smart contracts.

a. They are *decentralised*, meaning there is no central authority controlling them
b. They are *autonomous*, meaning they can operate with no human intervention
c. And they are *organisations*, meaning they have a structure and a purpose

DAOs differ from other organisations in a few ways. That DAOs operate with no human intervention means they make their own decisions and operates without human help. Imagine all the paperwork needed to govern a traditional company, the lawyers needed to negotiate terms and specify agreements, the administrative task of registering important events and the lack of transparency new investors have when considering a stock to be part of their portfolio.

Because DAOs are run by smart contracts, processes and transactions are carried out instantly, with 100% transparency and accountability (there are still some hiccups making this work but we'll get there).

My point here is that human interpretation, emotional resistance, errors, procrastination, and delays are eliminated. This may sound like a two-edged sword and even scary. However, the smart contract that determines how the DAO will be governed is after all created by humans and not some mystical robot.

The difference here is that a potential investor in the DAO will have full transparency into all decisions made and all governance protocols. If you want to invest in the stock market, you have, in reality, very little information to base your decision on - and they are often limited to past financial performance.

* * *

One of the primary uses of DAOs is for governance and voting. Everyone who takes part in the DAO has a say in how it operates. Because they are decentralised and autonomous, they can be used to make decisions about anything that affects the organisation. This can include things like what products to produce, how to spend the organisation's funds, who should be elected to the board of directors or whether to accept a new member into the community. Voting can be done through a web portal or by using a mobile app.

To vote in a DAO, you must be a member of the organisation. This usually means that you have to own some tokens that are used by the DAO. These tokens can be used to vote on proposals or participate in online discussions. Imagine a movie production being set up as a DAO with employees and other stakeholders being the owners of the DAO. They could have a say in how to produce the movie, how the story should end, and be entitled to a share of the overall profits if they did a great job and the movie becomes an international success.

Some platforms allow DAOs to vote on proposals submitted by third-party developers. This allows the DAO to take advantage of the ideas and expertise of people outside of the organisation.

* * *

As an author and publisher, you can create your own DAO and use it to build a powerful community around your work. If you commit to solving a problem in the world, you could create a DAO and let other people who are passionate about that subject and who feel they can contribute to the solution enter the DAO. The value of the token at the time of the entry will help finance the project - and for the investor, there is an incentive to help raise that value for a higher return.

What are social tokens?

Social tokens are a type of cryptocurrency. While cryptocurrencies like Bitcoins or Ether (also called crypto coins) are universal and can be used anywhere, social tokens (or creator tokens or creator coins) are digital cash to be used with your own community.

Yes, I know.... So many terms but you'll get there (therefore, I added the vocabulary at the end of the book).

If you want to remember two things only about social tokens, it should be that they are designed to incentivise participation in online communities and that their use is limited to the creator's community. Technically, any store could decide to accept payment with your tokens but since it's probably only a small part of their customers that hold your token, it's unlikely that others will implement your token as a payment option.

Content creators, such as YouTubers or bloggers, often use the tokens to monetize their work and engage their audience. They can, for example, be used to buy goods and services within the network or to access exclusive content. The value of social tokens comes from the networks they are used in. The more people use a social token, the more valuable it becomes.

You can think of them as quite similar to loyalty points or rewards points, but they can be traded on crypto marketplaces. I can't go anywhere to sell my gym membership or the miles I earned from American Airlines. But I can sell the social tokens I earned from reading your books or winning a contest you held. If there is a limited supply of your tokens and they are popular among your fans, I might profit from such sales. In that way, social tokens are assets that come in a digital form and represent a value that is in high or low demand, just like other assets.

You can set it up so fans can buy the token i.e. on Rally.io (and get visibility in that marketplace). Or you can give your community tokens as rewards for their activity. You participate in this event and earn coins. You listen to this podcast and earn coins. You read my book and earn coins. You pull in a new community member and earn coins. You get the idea. Do whatever makes sense in your community and for your business.

The buyer can use the coins to tip the creator, access exclusive parts of the community, or even become a co-creator or decision maker. This allows content creators to build closer relationships with their fans, as they are incentivised to participate in the community.

* * *

Now, reading about the social tokens, you might have asked yourself, how this is related to the influence DAO members have. And you are right, there is an overlap here. There are different types of social tokens, two of which seem most relevant for authors and publishers[38]:

1. *Personal tokens* (issued and controlled by an individual, i.e. a content creator)
2. *Community tokens* (issued and controlled by a group, i.e. a DAO)

Social tokens are distinct from *security tokens*. Social tokens are used to incentivise participation in online communities, while security tokens represent an investment in a company or project. The value of security tokens comes from the underlying asset they are linked to. This could be a physical asset, such as real estate or art, or it could be a financial asset, such as a company's earnings or a share of its profits. Social tokens are called social tokens or creator tokens because the asset is the creator and the social engagement.

Almost all business owners have experienced that social media platforms are very much pay-to-play platforms and you'll get very limited results without advertising. Here is the kicker; Social tokens can help authors, musicians, artists, and companies stay connected to their audiences without depending on social media platforms.

Social tokens are specific to the community and if they are used i.e. to give access to special perks, genuine fans will *hold on* to them. If you are a Banana Savannah fan or an Ed Sheeran fan, I bet you'd be happy to receive - or buy - social tokens that secured a front seat or backstage ticket. I'm sure you would probably love that! Even if you had to learn more about what social tokens are and can do.

As Jesse Cole comes up with even more crazy ideas like the Banana Nanas or publishes another bestselling book, the value of holding the token increases. More people want in. Since social tokens are an asset the holder owns, they can also choose to sell them on secondary markets.

But if members of the community love the brand and believe even more value will be added over time, it is likely they will hold on to the tokens and want to engage in the community and contribute to making it even more amazing.

They will most likely help attract more people by proudly speaking of the benefits of being a token holder. This will drive the value further up. Social tokens hold the potential to be an instrument not only to increase community value but to share that increased value with the community itself, giving them a financial incentive to creatively engage, help build the culture, and help the community grow. And as more people are attracted, the social tokens build social capital and financial capital simultaneously.

The internet hasn't happened yet

Wrapping up Part 1 of this book, I want to stress that I am aware of how easy it is to ignore these trends and find excuses why it's too soon to bother understanding what is happening or how it will open up opportunities for you. Some will also think it won't ever apply to their business or their audience. To that, I want to say, you also didn't think you would ever use a computer and you probably didn't own a carphone back in the days before smartphones.

Allow me to be frank with you. I am all smiles and full of love and compassion when saying this: If the world's biggest and most profit-focused organisations heavily invest, it will be your reality too. Your choice is between getting in early and learning while there is forgiveness and a real chance to turn the spotlight to you - or to wait until it's a catching-up game and the most you can achieve is to not be last and become mainstream.

In a Crypto Business podcast interview[39], historian Josh Rosenthal explains the historic evidence for his claim that the internet hasn't even happened yet. What happened in the Medieval and Renaissance is like what is happening again right now. Web3 is not just a new technology but a historic event, we are amid.

Now this part gets weird but bare with me because he has a point. Consider your Medieval twins life: You work dust to dawn, you work hard, you own nothing, you don't have access to information, you can't move far from your home, the world is flat. There were powerlords who decided for you. Money control was centralised with very few people controlling how much money was available. You didn't mentally have framework to understand the change that was just around the corner.

So what drives history? Renaissance means 'birth' or 'recreation' and it was very successful because of two technological inventions that changed everything: The ledger and the Gutenberg printing press. The ledger-based bookkeeping allowed finances to flow freely. With the ledger came microloans and trading balances. It was the introduction of 'debit' and 'credit' to regular people. You could now start a business without going to a centralised powerbroker but you could get a peer-to-peer loan. It is also called the birth of capitalism.

The idea of a printing press was terrible if you think about it. People couldn't read, only 5% was literate. But what happened was it created the possibility to spread information quickly and decentralised. Most of the content was small memes, and visuals that told the story. This made information, for the first time, available to the masses.

The printing press became the technology that enabled the ledger technology to spread like wildfire, because it educated people about how to use ledgers. The combination of technologies rebirthed and redefined society. The renaissance brought new art, a new power system, new ways of ownership, new autonomy - but more importantly, centralised powerholders couldn't stop this decentralisation change from happening.

Rosenthal describes how history happens slow, slow, slow, and then fast. It goes through predictable phases: aggregation, consolidation, decentralisation. We are definitely at the end of consolidation with all the problems related to that. The ledger and printing press decentralised and cracked down hierarchies.

Historians will look back and say the internet hasn't really happened yet (with web2) because we are still in consolidation. In the Medieval, 10% owned 90% of property. Information was filtered by those who also owned the capital. That's very similar to now. The few in power harvest the fruit from your interaction and contribution (you are the product).

With web3, we are looking at:

- A new ledger: Crypto is a decentralised way to share value, pay for things, send money - no middleman needed. Web3 gives the small man ownership - also to the protocols that run the system. You get *paid* for owning and using your token by participating in the community.

- A new printing press: There is no corporation, bank, social media platform or other intermediary that controls how you can take part or communicate. Instead of businesses paying platforms to reach audiences, they give out small pieces of their company to their community and make everyone a co-owner.

Change usually happens in 2 waves. First, people use technology to do the same only a little bit better. Second, they use technology to create things we couldn't even imagine before. Our Medieval twin wouldn't be able to imagine the changes of the Renaissance. Likewise, it's hard to wrap our head around what web3 will make possible.

History happens in small and bigger circles. Web1 and web2 were smaller circles that allowed us to do things and access things faster. And if you look at the timeline, digital networks started with the ARPANET in the 1960s as a way for government researchers to share information, and it wasn't until 1983 that the various networks shared the same protocol, creating what we call the internet, then used only by early adopters. It has only been mainstream for about 20 years.

Web3 technology is not new either, as you have seen earlier in this chapter. And it follows the same path as other historical major changes, like the renaissance. The new financial ledger (first Bitcoin) has been around for 15 years and it is now becoming mainstream. Then it moves into art and culture (which we see with the NFTs), then it moves into business (the very reason for writing this book) and becomes an economic engine for societal change.

There is no way around it. Web3 is a fundamental, transformative change, that will change all the same things that changed almost 800 years ago (Gutenberg printing press invented in 1450). Web3 is a cultural, political and economic rebirth - even an artistic rebirth.

Google, Amazon and Facebook are threatened by this. They are the authorities and intermediaries that these technologies are trying to eliminate. Add banks to that, who with few exceptions, are refusing transactions related to buying crypto currency. They are all now trying to either hinder web3 from happening or to bridge their businesses to the new world. Facebook is working on what internally is nicknamed the Zuck Buck, and with rebranding to Meta they send a strong signal that they will enable the change (or even that they are the change, which is not the case - the metaverse is not Facebook's). All social platforms are far into their NFT projects and finding ways to transition into the metaverse.

Corporate brands like Adidas, Nike, and Nissan, and celebrity brands like Johnny Depp, Snoop Dogg, Paris Hilton and Gary Vaynerchuk, and so many more are already heavily invested in web3.

It's not a matter if web3 is relevant to you. It's here and the game of business and publishing and owning content is already changing and it's one of the most impactful changes we have ever seen - and moving faster than ever.

Alright, let's look at what NFTs are, why people care about them and some actual ways to use them. The purpose of part 1 was to give you an insight into what is happening, create a sense of urgency to learn about web3, and introduce some of the major elements for web3. I saved NFTs for the next part, because it's the easiest way for you to start publishing your book in new ways and rethinking your relationship with readers.

PART 2
The Power Of NFTs

*How sweet. Now artists can become
little capitalist assholes as well.*

- **BRIAN ENO**, BRITISH MUSICIAN, COMPOSER,
RECORD PRODUCER AND VISUAL ARTIST

CHAPTER 4
Non-fungible tokens

What are NFTs?

Let me start by saying that if you have never heard about NFTs, there is nothing weird in that. While the first NFTs saw the light of the day in 2017, they first boomed in popularity in the beginning of 2021. You are not late but early into the world of NFTs with a tremendous opportunity to ride a rising wave and have people listen, because you are cooler than most now ;)

In technical terms, NFTs are cryptographic assets on blockchain with *unique identification codes* and *metadata* that distinguish them from each other.

Blockchain technology allows for a secure and transparent way to create and manage these unique assets, and even though it all sounds very nerdy, you can learn to create NFTs without too much effort. You can also trade NFTs, easily transfer ownership, make payments, and complete the transaction within minutes. This tricky part is not to use NFTs but to figure out what you want to use them for.

NFTs differ from the social tokens mentioned in chapter 3. Social tokens are a great way to engage a community and reward members for their participation. But they are like a local currency that can only be used within the realm of the creator. NFTs are not tied to any specific platform. They are digital assets that can be used anywhere.

But the biggest difference is that social tokens are fungible, whereas NFTs are non-fungible. Fungible means all social tokens from the same creator are alike. Therefore some creators reward with social tokens. Each token is not unique just like a dollar bill isn't unique. Imagine if I earned 1,000 of your creator coins and they all needed to be stored in my digital wallet. I might not be super keen on getting more of your coins. Therefore some creators reward with tokens and when reaching certain levels, the tokens can be converted to an NFT.

* * *

NFTs can represent real-world assets such as real estate, cars, and even art collections. They can also represent digital assets such as website domains, social media accounts, and online courses. Soon, we will see NFTs representing more abstract assets such as loyalty points, carbon credits, and even votes (which might, as mentioned, be earned as tokens and then converted to NFTs when reaching certain levels).

The visual representation of an NFT is a digital image or icon. However, they can also be represented by other means, such as video, QR codes or audio files. They are usually created by businesses or individuals who own the digital asset that they want to represent. For example, an artist may create an NFT to represent an art piece. A game developer may create an NFT to represent a virtual good in an online game.

* * *

Creating an NFT is done through a process called *minting* which will create a unique record of the digital asset on the blockchain. Minting an NFT requires the payment of a fee, called a gas fee. The size of the fee depends on which blockchain is being used and how many transactions miners in the blockchain network are processing at the specific time the mining takes place.

There is no doubt NFTs provide a way for creators to monetise their work in a new and innovative way. Once an NFT is created, it can be bought and sold like any other asset. Many online marketplaces allow the buying and selling of NFTs, the most popular ones being Opensea and Rarible.

* * *

This segways us into rarity. Now, rarity covers two different things. Most commonly, rarity refers to differences in the digital art for each NFT in a collection. In a collection of 1,111 NFTs there might only be one that features the creator herself. Or maybe only 3 of them have a golden star in the image and provide special privileges. The metadata features a rarity score which measures the combined rarity of multiple rare or less rare elements.

The price of an NFT depends on its rarity and of course also its popularity. NFTs can sell for absurdly high prices, sometimes even millions of dollars, depending on the perceived value and rarity of the asset, and the market conditions at the time of purchase. Unfortunately, these extreme cases have put all attention on NFTs as digital art collections - which often have very little utility and are all about the digital art.

I believe this will soon be reversed so that utility (what the NFT can do) comes first, and the digital art is less significant. This is the reason NFTs have their own part of this book; they deserve to be understood for their usefulness.

* * *

It goes beyond the purpose of this book to explain how exactly you buy and sell NFTs. There are lots of free resources out there to teach you this.

But I will share this:

1. *You need a digital wallet (could be MetaMask)*
2. *Create an account on an NFT marketplace, i.e. Opensea, Rarible or Superrare.*
3. *Find something cheap to buy to get familiar with the process (you can pay with crypto or credit card)*
4. *Create a Coinbase account in either case and say yes to notifications on currencies so you can buy when the rate is low*

Disclaimer: This is not financial advice and you should do your own research or seek professional advice.

* * *

NFT is right now not a commodity and trading happens on specialised marketplaces. However, you can already also buy them on eBay (at the time of writing this book, there were

1,113 Art NFTs for sale), and I have little doubt Amazon will get into the game soon, too, to offer a marketplace for NFTs. There are also several tech startups working on creating NFT book marketplaces where readers can buy and sell NFT books. These platforms are also offering associated publishing services for authors.

The financial sector is also paying attention. By August 2022, VISA announced they are launching a NFT Creator programme to support entrepreneurs building businesses using NFTs[40].

Retailers like Starbucks[41], Puma, Adidas, and Nike have all committed to NFTs[42]. In fact, Starbucks just announced the introduction of a reward system that will potentially introduce millions and millions of coffee drinkers to web3[43]. And Shopify offers token-gated commerce (part of the shop is hidden and only revealed to NFT holders): 'Connect with your fans and drive sales by giving token holders exclusive access to your merch, experiences, and more.'[44]

Even the UK Government announced in April 2022 that it is minting its own NFT[45] with the intent to 'show the forward-looking approach we are determined to take towards crypto assets in the UK'. They followed the announcement with a list of plans for the UK to regulate stablecoins and become a crypto asset hub.[46]

I find it mindblowing how quickly all of this has happened. It's not important if you got all the details. My mission is to show you, NFTs are the real deal and it's not going away any time soon.

Now, there is no market if there are no buyers. And I know you are likely asking yourself, why anyone would be interested in your NFT. Let's look at the many reasons why people buy NFTs. You need this information to create your own strategy.

Why people buy NFTs

Well, first of all, people *do* buy NFTs. Trading volume of NFTs in 2021 was over $17 billion, an increase of over 20,000% from 2020[47] and there are many reasons people might choose to buy an NFT.

The use cases for NFTs are only limited by our imagination and possibilities are endless. So far, we've only scratched the surface of what's possible and it's an exciting time to be involved in the world of NFTs and blockchain technology, also for you as an author or publisher. Before you consider how you will offer NFTs as part of your business or authorship, you should carefully consider your audience's motivation and let that shape your NFT project.

* * *

For some people, maybe they appreciate the design or artistry of the digital art piece. They have a *collectors* mindset and might also or in the past have collected other rare items like stamps, posters, cartoons, concert tickets, boarding passes from their summer vacations, or rare books. Perhaps they enjoy collecting things that have sentimental value or are fun, beautiful, rare, or unique. Oftentimes, they spend lots of time researching, studying and engaging in communities with like-minded people.

I feel confident guessing that you also once collected trading cards (basketball, baseball, soccer, cars, pokemon, etc.) - or maybe vinyl records or succulents? If you have children or grandchildren, you will also know the collector mindset is very much alive.

Sometimes collectors are superfans of a specific person or group and collect many different (all!) items available. They might even engage in designing items for that person or group. To keep this group engaged, an NFT product must address variety, rarity and often, scarcity. In return, superfans might (proudly) display their collection online, thereby giving visibility and credibility to your brand.

A great example from earlier this year is the NFL partnering with Ticketmaster to provide a complementary NFT ticket to everyone who purchases a ticket. Each ticket is unique because it is for a specific game, a specific date, and for a specific seat. Imagine how excited a true fan would be, to show off the highest amount of tickets, or the best seating, in their Instagram feed (because you can do that now, showing your NFTs in your Insta-feed) or on their fanblog[48].

* * *

Others may view the purchase of an NFT as more of an *investment*, betting that the value of the NFT will increase. They might purchase an NFT with the intent to sell it at a later date.

Some people in this category are in it for speculation - they're hoping to get in early on the next big thing and cash out before the bubble bursts. Like when Sina Estavi paid almost $3 million for an NFT of the first-ever Tweet with the expectation to resell it at a profit.

Others believe in the team creating the NFT and want to sponsor their project besides a potential financial gain. The Crypto Tech Women NFT is an example of that. The CTW collection minted on February 26, 2022 and sold out within 24 hours of our public sale. The organisation's mission is to empower, educate and help everyone join the web3 space. Many of the investors, including yours truly, invested to support the mission, believing in the team behind the project. Time will tell if it pays off as a financial investment, but I was happy about the attention the project got and the resulting number of women learning more about web3[49].

The project was a so called PFP project (Picture for Proof/ Profile)[50], a type of NFT project that has been very popular in the past year. A PFP will create a collection of images that have common properties but are all different. The Bored Apes Yacht Club (BAYC), Cryptopunks, and Gary Vaynerchauks VeeFriends are the most widely known - and most profitable - PFP projects.

How does it work? You create, let's say 777 NFTs, each with a unique image. Like mentioned earlier, some properties will be rarer than others. People will then buy one of the NFTs during what we can describe as an auction. Hopefully, more people want to buy NFTs than there are NFTs available. The first buyers will often buy more than one since they expect to sell some of the NFTs again on the secondary market. Surpriiiise... the price goes up over time as long as people expect it to. Also, NFT-owners will help to build the value and demand - because it's in their own best interest.

To make a PFP project successful requires you either already have significant interest from your significant audience or that you find partners who will help you promote to larger communities. Or you can make the PFP project at a small scale and for example use quotes from the book (like Mark Manson's NFTs, The Subtle Art of Not Giving a F*ck - he created a lot though), images of characters from your novel, pieces of the front cover, or whatever you want. The point is you should limit the amount of NFTs to be lower than you think you can sell.

* * *

You can also create a pre-order campaign for your book, promising all buyers a special edition of the book and maybe some perks along with an NFT to show your appreciation. Another way of doing this is to create a so called whitelist for your NFT and relate it to a book topic you are thinking about. If people sign up for the whitelist, your book must be a good idea.

You should in both cases talk about how you plan to add value to the NFT. This way, the purpose of your NFT is *crowdfunding*, and investors will likely be people who believe in you or are already in your network and curious to learn about NFTs.

Finally, some people buy NFTs for what they can do, for their *utility value*. This topic is more extensive and I devoted the entire next chapter to it.

CHAPTER 5
What can NFTs do?

Proof of originality

To start with an example that might help you grasp how NFTs can help document ownership and origin, think of the significant problems luxury brands experience with copycats. If I buy a Louis Vuitton bag in a flagship store, I can be almost certain, it's an authentic LV bag. If I buy one from a salesman in the street in a touristy beach town in Spain or at the Yellow Market in Beijing, I can be pretty sure it's fake. But what if I buy it on a secondary market, like eBay?

As mentioned, the blockchain is a public, decentralised database that records all transactions (buying and selling, but also so much more as you will learn in this chapter).

The block can also not be duplicated and the documentation not be changed or otherwise tampered with. So what a person is buying when buying an NFT, is a public record on the blockchain that proves that they are the owner of that specific asset.

That it is public means that everyone can see which wallet the NFT belongs to. You can't always see who the wallet belongs to but you can think of the wallet number as the unique web3 ID, like the email often is in web2.

It is all transparent. You can look up a person's Opensea account and see which NFTs they own, how much they paid for their NFTs, and which wallet held the NFT before. And you can, in a matter of seconds, track it all the way back to the original creator.

Could the seller on eBay not just show me any Louis Vuitton NFT and say it's theirs? No, because only the actual owner of the NFT has the NFT in *his* wallet and only he can transfer it to me (which then creates a new block in the chain, documenting I am now the owner). By reviewing the records, I would be able to follow all transactions on that specific bag and identify if the original creator of the NFT was, in fact, Louis Vuitton.

Even if this documentation won't stop people from copying the product, it gives honest people a way to know what they are paying for. Being able to document originality is likely to offer a higher reselling price. And if the product is or becomes a rare item, the price might even increase.

Duplicated originals

Let's say you're an artist and want to sell your latest painting. Now, it's obvious that each real-world, physical painting created by an artist is a unique product that can only be sold once. I think you'd also agree that we can copy a digital piece of art an infinite number of times with no loss in quality.

The hard part to wrap your head around is that each digital art piece is, in fact, unique - even though the visual representation is the same. "How can that be?", you might ask. I am glad you asked because that is one of the key features of an NFT.

It comes back to what we just talked about: Each created NFT adds a unique block to the chain, providing a record of ownership. What people are buying is that specific record. This means that if you create 100 NFTs based on that same art piece, they are still all unique products. The artwork is just the visual representation of the unique block added to the blockchain.

But why would anyone want to buy that?

Well, you could say that there are even enough people in the world who would buy a piece of art they know is fake. This is not the case here though. These are visually alike but all authentic.

Some people will buy because they are collectors, or because they believe in you as an artist, or want to support you, or someday want to own the physical version. Or the NFT comes with other perks, like a free ticket to your next exhibition or a course that teaches how to [whatever you teach].

For authors, you can sell your digital book (or course) as an NFT. We call this a *digital original* and we will come back to how you can look differently at your book as a product, in chapter 7.

Airdrops to increase value

In today's world, it's very unlikely that the value of a paperback or hardback will increase after the first time it's sold. Think of all that great stories and knowledge stored on bookshelves - providing no further value to the world, maybe except for emotional value revoked when the eye catches the title on the spine, or the more psychological value of displaying in your home that you are a vivid reader.

But unless you resell for a fraction of the price in a secondary market or give it away, no more eyes will reach the words of the pages inside it. The content just sits there. The words will ignite no more brains. No more imagination is created. No more knowledge is transferred to people who need it. Some people will read their book again some time or use it to look up something they once read, but for most books, they are read, stored on the bookshelf and only if it was extremely helpful, the reader might look up the author and connect, but mostly they'd be too intimidated to even have the thought it's possible. The author remains a mystery, an unreachable icon.

* * *

As an author, you have no means to *increase* the value or enhance the experience for the reader after the initial purchase (unless you get them to join your email list and they open those).

One of the most exciting features of NFTs is that their value is not *only* determined by the market but can be influenced by the creator over time in at least two ways:

a. The creator can create a higher *demand* for a limited number of NFTs as the creators brand becomes more widely known and more people become emotionally connected to it.

b. The creator can increase the *experienced value* of the NFT by adding more content, features, rights and other utilities to it over time.

The latter is very interesting for authors. NFTs give you a way to reach your readers in a new way. You will know who owns your NFTs at any point in time, even if they are resold multiple times. And you can add new content and privileges to the NFT. This could be a new version of your book, an exclusive bonus chapter, behind the scenes video or an invitation to your next 2-day workshop.

There are different technical ways of getting that new content or privileges to the NFT holders and it goes beyond the purpose of this book to go into detail. Just know that sometimes, the NFT holder will need to discover new drops themselves by checking in to a NFT holder webpage that outlines the total list of privileges, or by participating in the community associated with your NFT. Sometimes, you would drop a new NFT to them and 'burn' the old. It would make sense that you could push this out directly to the existing NFT. My guess is that you will soon be able to do that and even make it part of the metadata in the NFT block. There are companies like Salesforce who are working on 'listening' tools that can identify accounts that are likely to be interested in a free drop. It's not without complications but I am sure airdropping will be further developed in the near future.

* * *

Airdropping holds the potential not only to increase the value of the NFT in the secondary market (incentivising people to resell it at a higher price) but also to engage readers in your work and create an anchor for what they might think you will do in the future (incentivising them to hold on to the NFT).

Either way, you win a much wider attention span with the reader. They won't just read and store. They will track the development, engage with more of your content (and hopefully, your business), and because this is a new an exciting experience, they will most likely tell even more people about what you do and become loyal fans and ambassadors - or if they intend to sell their NFT at a profit, seek out those fans for you to drive demand up.

Process execution

Behind the NFT artwork (the image that represents your NFT), is a *smart contract*. I mentioned earlier that what NFT buyers really buy is the record on the blockchain, not the artwork. That's important for the documentation part. But for the utility part (what the buyer can *do* with the NFT), what you pay for is what is in the underlying smart contract.

Smart contracts are small computer programs that live on the blockchain and execute whatever is in the contract when certain conditions are met. In the following, I outline different categories. The list is not a complete overview. The possibilities are only limited by our imagination.

Provide or restrict access

When I purchased my 'Crypto Tech Women' NFT, they also granted me access to a learning platform teaching (women) how to create NFTs and a whole lot more. All I need to do is to go to their website, connect my digital wallet, and the protocol will look up on the blockchain if I own the necessary NFT to unlock the content.

This functionality is called a *tokengate* - and I am sure you will see these pop up everywhere real soon. In fact, I am considering including that in the Single Sign-On for my membership. You know, when you can log in with your Facebook or Google account. You will also be able to choose to connect to your digital wallet and confirm you own one of my NFTs.

In time, tokengates are also likely to replace loyalty cards. You might hold an annoying number of loyalty cards from Starbucks, Amazon, BestBuy, and more. A tokengate would allow you to connect to their communities if you hold their token in your digital wallet. One point of touch for you; your wallet. One unique identification you can use across platforms instead of a gazillion email logins.

That same NFT might give you access to chat groups, future events, exclusive customer service levels, first access or exclusive access to new products, etc. Even access to a next round of NFTs, or a dinner with the author.

You can also connect it to exclusive offers, to get a discount on your next book, or provide access to content not shared elsewhere. To come up with more ideas, you can let yourself be inspired by how movies or series sometimes offer bonus material with more in-depth info or from-clips. When I purchased my Mark Manson NFT, they gave me access to an unreleased chapter.

Royalties from secondary markets

Now that you learned to think about the NFT as a relationship you have with the NFT holder through the wallet address, let's assume the creator is fantastic at adding value to the NFT, then maybe demand for the NFT will also increase. When the NFT holders see (the market being completely transparent) that other NFT holders sell their NFTs at a profit, they might consider selling too.

Now after all the time you as the creator have spent building that additional value, should you then be dissatisfied that people choose to cash in and sell their NFT?

First of all, don't read too much into it. They might have purchased more than one (or you *gave* them more than one) *because they had faith in you!!*

Also, that they are selling their NFT, does not mean they aren't loyal fans or won't still be customers in your business or buy another NFT at a later point. They are not selling because they don't believe in you but because you proved your worth to them.

But the point I want to make here is that your very strategy might be to *inspire* people to sell your NFTs as many times as possible. Passing that value along to as many people as possible, you will not only reach more people who are willing to invest in what you offer, you can even make money from each transaction. How about that?!

You can program into the smart contract, that a certain percentage of the sales price for each sale, should go to *your* digital wallet. You can also assign royalty privilege to the cover designer, the illustrator, your mom, a charity organisation - or even give back to the community to incentivise them to help build even more value.

And when I say you can program it, you really just need to add the wallet addresses to the people who should be paid when the NFT shifts wallet. This way, you can earn industry-high royalties for first-time sales of your NFT book and royalties on secondary sales in perpetuity. *(NFT Bookstores usually offer royalties in perpetuity, even if it is not a technically perfect solution yet)*

* * *

There is something very unfortunate about how the publishing industry works today. Because authors and publishers are only compensated at the first sale, the entire industry is focused on selling *new* books. Bookstores like Amazon are realising there is a secondary market for used books. But creators (or publishers) get zero compensation from that.

Why do I think this is a problem? Well, it would only be fair that the mind and soul who created content that people found worth resharing, is paid for the real value of their work. But what I am aiming at here is the environmental impact of *overproduction of books.*

This stems not only from print books that are never sold and eventually destroyed (which is also a gigantic problem). I am not making the argument either, that you should deselect paper versions of your book or that fewer titles should be published as paperbacks or hardbacks.

Instead, I am highlighting the opportunity to create a higher demand for trading books, reader to reader, with proper compensation to the right people; those who created the book. NFTs make it possible to resell ebooks and audiobooks, and smart contracts make it easy to ensure that creators are receiving their cut (even if there is still development necessary to eliminate all ways to bypass this).

Instant compensation

One of my authors once asked me to help solve a technical problem with her account on the self-publishing platform she used to publish her book. She knew that her clients had purchased books but she had received no royalties.

After logging into her account, I could see nothing wrong. The reports showed more or less the number of books sold she had indicated. So I checked the payout section and found nothing wrong there either.

The 'problem' turned out to be her expectations. At no point was it part of her thinking that there might be policies stating a later payout time than immediately after the purchase.

And, there is no reason she shouldn't receive her share with no delay. She was already cleared to receive payouts when she created her publisher account. And the entire process from the customer ordering her book to the registration of the sale in her publisher account is 100% digital. No human is (or needs to be) involved. Yet, policies state she has to wait for months.

Royalties for books sold via KDP Amazon in May will be paid out to the author at the end of July. On other platforms, payout time will depend on the payout option you choose. Using PayPal, Lulu will offer payout by the end of the month.

‘

If you want a paper check, you'll have to wait 45 days after the end of the month.

With Ingramspark, payouts happen 90 days after the end of the quarter. And even though this sounds bad enough, it's a lot worse if you choose a traditional publisher. Payouts twice a year are not uncommon.

Pardon my French, but what the hell?! 6 months?! Sometimes even a lot longer. As if computers and the internet weren't invented yet. Not even weeks can be considered a necessity.

Therefore I am excited to share that NFT transactions are completed within minutes of the transaction happening, including paying the original creator whatever is stated in the smart contract.

CHAPTER 6
Ownership

Licensing rights

In a traditional approach, buying an NFT will not mean intellectual property (IP) is transferred. The creator has copyrights and rights to the commercial use of the content that comes with the NFT unless otherwise stated (including the NFT artwork).

In December 2021, Adidas AG released its "Into the Metaverse" collection. The terms and conditions states[51]:

- "You acknowledge and agree that Adidas AG owns all legal right, title and interest in and to the Art, and all intellectual property rights therein."
- "Adidas grants you a worldwide, non-exclusive, revocable, royalty-free license, to display the Art for your Purchased NFTs, solely for the following purposes:
  - (i) for your own personal, non-commercial use (for example home display, display in a virtual gallery or as an avatar); or
  - (ii) as part of a marketplace that permits the purchase and sale of your NFTs."

They could have taken it a step further (like Nike subsidiary RTFKT), and permit NFT owners to use the underlying IP

85

of their NFT to create and sell physical merchandise with the NFT artwork displayed on it[52]. Or they could go full monty and not only permit the NFT owner all commercial rights but transfer the underlying IP.

This is what the extremely successful NFT project (Yuga Labs LLC) did. They created an NFT collection of 10,000 unique "Bored Ape" NFTs. Celebrities (including Justin Bieber, Jimmy Fallon, Paris Hilton and Eminem) and Adidas have all acquired their own Bored Ape NFT, now owning not only the NFT but also the underlying asset and IP[53] as stated in the terms:

- "Each Bored Ape is an NFT on the Ethereum blockchain. When you purchase an NFT, you own the underlying Bored Ape, the Art, completely. Ownership of the NFT is mediated entirely by the Smart Contract and the Ethereum Network: at no point may we seize, freeze, or otherwise modify the ownership of any Bored Ape."
- Yuga Labs LLC grants you an unlimited, worldwide license to use, copy, and display the purchased Art for the purpose of creating derivative works based upon the Art."

Owners have used their Bored Apes in movies, music, podcasts, books, streetwear and more.

Voting

The smart contract can also create voting rights. This will allow holders of the NFTs to vote on certain proposals or issues. Using NFTs for voting can help to reduce fraud and increase transparency. It is much more difficult to forge NFTs than traditional ballots and NFTs can track the results of a vote in real-time, making it impossible to manipulate the results. You can do an NFT voting in a public or private manner, depending on your preferences.

We can use voting rights at different levels. If the NFT is tied to a Decentralised Autonomous Organisation (DAO, see chapter 3), you can allow the DAO's members to participate in the decision-making process and *influence the value of their investment.*

If you are looking to give voting rights to fans with the purpose of *enhancing their fan experience*, you could give voting rights to:

a. Who should receive NFT-holder awards, best rookie award, or other awards to honour community-members who deserve recognition
b. Which content or new products to create
c. Location for a live event
d. Ideal speakers for a summit
e. Book cover
f. And more

Technically, there are no limitations to what you can do with your NFT. Your imagination is the limit.

Bring physical products into the Metaverse

To spark your imagination of what is possible, you can use NFTs to bring a physical product into the Metaverse. Imagine you purchased the Louis Vuitton, you always wanted and received a complementary NFT. Louis Vuitton might then allow you to add that bag to your digital avatar in the Metaverse, making it part of your digital identity.

If you live in a developed country, chances are you spend money on 'stuff' that only people who visit you in your home will ever know you own. Now, you can flash it all as part of your digital identity online. And if you can't personally relate to that, just think about what people choose to show on their social media. Soon, they will dress their digital avatar up (which lives across different platforms) to reflect who they are as a person - or as a secondary identity.

* * *

Bringing it back to publishing and your authorship, you could create a unique special edition of your book, signed by the author and with a unique, personal message to the reader. You tie the book to an NFT and allow the person to bring it to reading clubs or to hang on their digital book display in their own space in the Metaverse.

* * *

It may feel like a steep learning curve to figure out how to carry out projects like this. I encourage you to seek counselling to ensure your intent, strategy and legal/financial risks are aligned, and the smart contract is designed to execute as intended.

I want you to remember that we are at the beginning of the web3 era and thousands and thousands of developers are right now developing services to help people use the new technologies. This includes services for publishers and authors and while writing this book, I discover new services every day (some more developed than others).

Soon this will be super easy to implement for you, and there are already lots of developer services available to help you with the tech part if you don't want to wait for the mainstream solution but take advantage of being early in this new market.

But the NFT landscape is already mature enough for me to publish this book as an NFT! Check out goosebump.pub/NFT to get your hands on one.

* * *

Now, let's bring it all together with a few examples of how NFTs have been used to raise funds, raise engagement and empower fans to create additional brand value….

USE CASE
BIG3 basket ball

BIG3 is a 3-on-3 basketball league founded by hip-hop musician and actor Ice Cube and entertainment executive Jeff Kwatinetz (note the artistic influence).

The league has 12 teams whose rosters include both former NBA players and international players. The rules deviate from official FIBA. In 2020, Big3 named the new basketball variant FIREBALL3[54].

BIG3 has taken a stand on issues like female coaches on male teams, inclusion, and that players are treated like people rather than just revenue-generating assets. In May 2022, they announced they also want to break down the wall between fans and decision makers in an ambitious NFT project.[55]

The nature of relationships between fans and sports teams in general is purely transactional. You pay to stream and watch at home or you pay more to watch the game in-person. The more you pay, the closer you will sit - and park. You can engage in discussions online, with your friends, or the guy sitting next to you. But you have no influence on the play, even if you think it helps yelling louder from the 30th row.

BIG3 offered 1,000 superfans to go "past engagement and into an empowering experience". There were 975 'Gold tier' NFTs available at $5,000 each and 25 'Fire tier' NFTs at $25,000 each. Depending on which tier you hold, you will get access to a quite extraordinary experience which, among many other benefits, include:

a. Reserved Owner Suites with A-Level Catering, reserved VIP Owners Seating Section, and backstage access area, VIP parking, special entrance etc.

b. Player and coach meet-and-greets, attendance to press conferences, attendance to parties with players and league personnel, meet-and-greets with players and coaches, pre-draft day party, invites to practices etc.

c. Access to weekly calls with your team to talk strategy leading up to each game, weekly video calls with referees to discuss rules and how you think their calls impacted the last game, opportunity to connect with commissioner Clyde Drexler, as well as league founders Jeff Kwatinetz and Ice Cube, three times a year to discuss fundamental strategy, changes, and ideas for the league

d. Voting on a number of matters

I encourage you to read the full article referenced. (#54 in the endnotes list). It's full of ideas and tells the complete story behind the NFTs.

USE CASE
Johnny Depp

The collection 'Never Fear Truth' was developed from original artwork by Johnny Depp[56], which has been embellished and animated into 11,111 NFTs which were launched at the beginning of 2022. The art pieces are the first ever published by Depp.

It features portraits of his friends and heroes, including Marlon Brando, Elizabeth Taylor, Depp's late dog Mooh, Depp himself, and a fictional character created by his son (in his dreams), called Bunny Man. The digital art pieces are gorgeous. Recognisable images of people in vibrant, bright colours. Pop Art overlayed with the energy and wit of Street Art.

One interesting aspect of the project is that it donates 25% of all proceeds to charities either supported by Depp or close to the subjects within the artwork. People can join the community on Discord, engage in the project, and have a say in which projects to support or, collaborate on creative projects.

The released holder benefits include a unique physical print of your NFT artwork, shipped to you at the cost of production and delivery. It will include your unique NFT# and Johnny Depp's official art certification.

If you hold the Bunny Man NFT, you can send a sketch of a carrot and it'll be incorporated into a physical Bunny Man artwork that is unique to both artists: you and JD. He'll then sign each of the original, physical works and send it back to you.

Both utilities are unique to NFT holders. You'll also get priority access to future NFT works and partnerships by Johnny Depp.

Now, you can say that Johnny Depp already had an enormous fan base and that he could have sold his out without the NFT. This would however, not have brought his committed creative fans together, the charity part would have been less significant and less transparent (since NFT transactions are public, we can all know how much was donated), and it certainly wouldn't have gained the same attention among other creators (which is a different segment than fans of his movies and music, even if there are overlaps).

PART 3
Authorship Reimagined

Imagination is more important than knowledge

- EINSTEIN

CHAPTER 7
Books reinvented

Will NFTs create a shift to digital books?

As briefly mentioned in chapter 5, NFT books are per definition originals. Even if 100 or 10,000 digital copies of the book are created, each book is registered (minted) on a blockchain providing the metadata of who published the book and when. This will not prevent pirate copies in the market but will provide evidence to the buyer that they are purchasing a legal copy for which the creator is compensated.

I mentioned that NFTs also make it possible for the reader to resell the book - perhaps even at a profit if the demand for the (limited number of) books has increased.

But will NFTs make digital formats more attractive to the reader? Yes and no. I think that if your audience has a collectors mindset, or if you have superfans, or if they are likely to see NFTs as an investment - they would be compelled to buy the digital book as an NFT if they believe they will receive additional value to the reading experience itself.

Or they might be interested because books feel like a familiar way to learn about this new technology. In fact, I think authors with an audience and the publishing industry should not underestimate the significance of timing here. Web3 is bursting through the surface and quickly becoming user-friendly even for less tech-savvy people.

Millions and millions of people will soon want to learn to navigate NFT marketplaces and understand how to create a digital wallet or how to use their NFT to unlock access to content, events, merchandise, metaverse spaces, and even social media. Whoever helps them effortlessly cross the threshold to this new world will earn their trust and gratitude.

But if we look at this as a reader's choice between print format and digital format, I don't think NFTs will make a difference. Not for the person in the role of a common reader. The reading experience will be the same as for an ebook purchased on Amazon, assuming the NFT is created in one of the specialised marketplaces and is delivered through an e-reader.

* * *

The better question is *how authors can use the digital format to make people interested in buying their NFTs* (regardless of what the author is looking to achieve with those NFTs). And I think they absolutely can - and from an environmental perspective, we probably should do a lot more to encourage people to buy the digital formats and do our part in reducing the overproduction of print books, while reaping the many other benefits of digital formats, like increased profits.

So how can we do that? It's really quite simple. We can create a more interesting offer, tie it to the NFT and only make it available as an NFT book. In chapter 8, I will come back to how to make it different through the content itself but for now,

I have a point to make about the underutilised features of the digital format.

An ebook is not the PDFs they offer you in somebody's marketing funnel. An ebook allows the reader to adjust the font and font size, or even change the background colour, so it's easier to read in the evening. The text is nowadays almost always in flow format and the amount of text on the screen will adjust to the size of the screen. This is also why ebooks don't have page numbers.

The layout should take into consideration how the reading experience will be, when turned into an ebook. There are certain graphic elements that don't work well with the ebook format. Unfortunately, most books are designed solely to make the print versions look stunning - or there isn't much thought behind the layout and it's all just plain text.

The reason an ebook has the functionality above is that it is programmed, just like a website which will also look different on a smartphone than on a bigger computer screen. Somehow we seem to forget that ebooks are digital and could do so much more than a print book can offer.

Ebooks can be *interactive* and make use of multiple types of content. Let me just first clarify that just because links are clickable it doesn't mean the book is interactive. There is some confusion about that. Interactive means that it is designed for *active reader participation*. They can include video, sound effects, gaming elements, or perhaps a calculator embedded in the book.

Authors entertain, teach, and shape our imaginations. Our job is not done just by writing the manuscript. We need people to want to open their minds and hearts to us. We need to creatively communicate our message and attempt to capture the attention of the reader - and *hold it* throughout the book.

People do love to read books. But we are all getting accustomed to visual and audio content. I think it's fair to assume that adding visual and audio elements to the ebook layout will make it more digestible to many readers. And using widgets (which are just little pieces of programming), you can create a much stronger learning experience.

There is nothing new in this. I created an interactive ebook 15 years ago. Yet, it is still not common practice at all. Most ebooks are considered 'practical' rather than unforgettable. And I believe that is the very reason print books still prevail. People buy ebooks to avoid carrying books around in their everyday life or during travels.

So, assuming you agree that reducing overproduction and giving people a reason to buy digital books instead of print is a good idea, what is needed to create that change?

Well, the technology to create amazing digital books is already there. But as mentioned, nothing much has happened for the past 15 years and honestly, publishers have taken their time to take the ebook format seriously - and the bookstores have worked against the common good by making their e-readers exclusive to specific formats and not allowing the reader to keep all of their purchases in the same app. Amazon has, for example, had its own file format until recently.

The thing is that the publishing industry largely consists of - excuse my frankness on this - dinosaur printing and rights trading businesses. They are not tech companies looking to invent the next amazing book format.

* * *

NFTs have brought new players into the game. The first author services to produce and sell NFT books based on interactive ebook formats are seeing the light of the day, created by progressive former publishers, marketers and tech people who see the opportunity to bypass traditional publishers and print-on-demand-based platforms completely.

These tech companies are building a *new industry* that is all about giving power back to the people, which includes both readers and creators.

Previously, there was no significant motivation to create amazing ebooks. Since they by many are considered a poorer experience, the opportunities were overlooked. And this brings me to what might be the real reason the ebook format will grow alongside the NFTs.

Those who develop NFT publishing services, the authors and the buyer of the NFT all have the *same incentive to create something of more value*: Higher experienced value equals higher trading prices. That also equals higher platform commission to the publishing platform, higher royalties to the author, and a potentially higher resell price for the reader.

The interactive format might hold the potential to serve as a motivator for you to make more money on your books and on your NFTs. I think this is especially true for nonfiction authors who are already focused on enhancing learning for their audience.

One script, many products

Our perception of what a book is hasn't changed much since 'Gutenberg Bible', the first book people would generally think of as a book. The book was printed by Johannes Gutenberg, who invented the printing press and started the Printing Revolution, around 1450 – 1455[57].

Even today, Oxford languages will define a book as "a written or printed work consisting of pages glued or sewn together along one side and bound in covers." Apart from the fact that neither digital ebooks nor audio is mentioned, it is clearly a fixed format meant to preserve stories and knowledge. Not optimised for learning or entertainment.

But humans have preserved stories and knowledge long before the book format. Perhaps the most natural format for humans is not the written word but visual communication like drawings and paintings, and oral transmissions like storytelling and song. If we look at which media is attracting more people today, these formats are still popular. Short video format and audio are far more popular than blogs.

People still do like long books though. In both the US, UK and Germany, a third of readers only read print format. 40-45% read a combination of print, audio and ebook and the rest of the readers read either ebooks or audio or a combination of two formats.

So unless we think a third of the market is enough for us (which is just crazy), there is little doubt that we should publish in as many formats as possible - and even add the interactive, multimedia format to the list.

However, there is so much more we can do, especially if we let go of the idea that print is more important than other formats. To optimise profits from print, we need higher volumes of each print. But that is not the case with digital formats.

We can create smaller 'editions' and limit how many copies of each book exist, using the NFTs. And we can turn our books into collectables or launch the book chapter by chapter and involve the audience in where the story is going or how the content is updated and kept accurate and current.

We can also create rare editions or multiple editions with different front covers, different endings, longer or more compressed versions, or books that are not linear but where the reader creates their own story by making choices throughout the book.

If you speak Spanish, you know the Spanish word for a book is 'libro'. It originates from the Latin word 'liber' which means free. We find this meaning also in words like library, deliver (b and v are used interchangeably in many Spanish cultures), liberate, and liberty.

To me, the very purpose of a book is to liberate knowledge and shape imagination so people can live their best lives and make their biggest contributions to a better world. Our job as authors is to creatively liberate our stories and knowledge so that many people can benefit from our work. We are teachers.

I can't help but wonder why we stick to a model that is hundreds of years old: One manuscript - one book. And if we go crazy: one book - three formats (paper, ebook, audio). A key skill for an author today is marketing. And if we look at this from a marketer's perspective, you would try different angles and cut the cake in different shapes to capture as big a part of the market as you can.

I suggest that we keep an open mind to what our readers (customers) want *and* what will capture their attention. A part of your audience is likely collectors. So give them something to collect. A part is likely into investing. So give them something to invest in. A part will prefer shorter formats. So give them a resume. A part will prefer to know the backstory. So give them bonus material. A part will prefer a visual presentation so provide videos or infographics. These things could be standalone products themselves, all based on the same initial work: your one manuscript.

Artificial intelligence (AI)

When reinventing books, we also need to look at how we create them and by this, I mean how we produce the actual text (or audio because you could create that first too).

About 50% of this book was written by Jasper, an AI robot that is trained to predict what you want to write next. Jasper has 'read' 10% of all content on the internet and based on the input and commands I give Jasper, it will create suggestions for text that is 99.999% original. There is no copying or plagiarism involved and Jasper never had a single dispute on that. I am the owner of the content and Jasper waves all copyrights to what I create. (*check terms for your specific platform, including terms for commercial use*)

There are many other similar AI tools like CopyMatic, Ryter, CopyAI, WriteSonic etc. Just to let you know how popular these tools are, I discovered WriteSonic because it showed up as the number 1 topic in 'Exploding Topics', which is a newsletter service that delivers insights on what people are talking about online right now.

Like many of the other technologies mentioned in this book, artificial intelligence is not new but is merely becoming more accessible to non-tech people now. What these AI writing tools use is big data. If the data pool is large enough, there will be patterns in which words people will use and how to describe certain phenomena or to tell stories.

In 2011, Watson and machine learning were on everybody's lips in the tech innovation space and I remember meeting with Microsoft to present an idea on how to use big data to enrich and build on ideas in our Idea Bank (yep, we believed in those back then).

The problem with innovation in big, old, popular companies is that there are mainly many ideas because they stack up over time and don't get implemented. They die because they are all heard before and are not potent enough to shake anyone's world.

We imagined big data and machine learning could add new information to the original idea and fuel discussions that would lead to better ideas that stood a chance to survive bureaucracy and the myopia any organisation like that suffers from. Microsoft loved the idea - but the idea didn't survive in our own organisation.

Watson was created as a "question answering (QA) computing system that IBM built to apply advanced *natural language* processing, information retrieval, knowledge representation, automated *reasoning*, and machine learning technologies to the field of *open domain question answering*"[58].

What I find fascinating about AI writing tools is the reasoning part. Using Jasper to write this book was an experiment and apart from speeding up the writing significantly, it also broadened my mind and brought matters to attention that I hadn't thought of before. It also found sources of information for me and perhaps most importantly, it did some of my research to find use cases that people in general find interesting.

Perhaps Google could help you with that. Sure, but Jasper does it much faster, with no agenda to promote certain content and using *reasoning* to predict which use cases will be the most relevant for this specific book. Suggestions are made based on what is already in my document and the questions I ask and the prompts I give for what content to look for. It also does not find other people's content, it creates original content I own. Jasper has indeed been what it's intended to be: An assistant I can instruct and guide using natural language as if I was talking to a human.

* * *

Your new AI toolbox to use as an author doesn't stop there. Jasper just launched another tool.[59] This tool will create original images based on your text prompts. The more precisely you describe what should be in the image and which style you are looking for, the more fantastic images it will create for you. Not find, but create. And Jasper is not alone in this field either. The internet is overflowing with images created using DALE-E 2 and Midjourney.

The cover illustration of this book is created by me using such AI tool. The output quality wasn't good enough for printing though. So what do you do? You use another AI tool to improve the quality and turn it into a high-resolution image more than ok for printing.

This means that you might not need a creative book cover designer to create a unique and eye-catching image anymore. Practising will make you better but in reality, you can create an original image within minutes or down to as little as 15 seconds. This means you can give a lot of tries in just 30 minutes between meetings or on the bus ride home. And you don't need any technical skills for either AI writing or AI image creation. Just practise in *asking* for what you want which is not that different from asking a human to create something original for you.

Maybe this will blow your mind. AI tools that will allow you to create videos based on text prompts are tested in beta and will soon viable to consider for your AI toolbox too.

* * *

Now, if you think it stops there, you are wrong. You can also have your audiobook recorded with no human reading the book.

Ups… let me back up there and just be clear about this: you should absolutely read out your book aloud before finishing up your script (to capture what won't sound great in the reader's head). You'll discover some necessary adjustments but why not record that reading in high-quality audio so you can turn it into your audio product. Just get a great less than $150 microphone and sit at the bottom of your closet and you have the perfect soundproof studio.

Soon, you'll be able to just upload your text file to some service online along with some audio or video with your voice in it - and it can create the perfect AI narrated audio file using your own voice.

Here is why I am convinced that is just around the corner:

1. You can already use tools like Descript not only to transcribe audio (and video) files in seconds or minutes but you can also change words in the text it creates and add it back into the original audio or video file - in your voice!

2. There are multiple AI narrating services available in the market already. You choose a voice from a catalogue and it will create the audio file with no human inter-action. For nonfiction authors looking to connect with their audience, I recommend you use your own voice if at all possible though.

3. Unrelated to AI, but as a side note, I want to also men-tion that you can record your book remotely with a professional studio and don't have to travel anywhere to record it yourself while you will still get the help of a professional production team.

* * *

Some of you will see red flags here. Who controls the algo-rithms and who is then shaping our imagination of what's possible? Others may think this way of creating books is 'cheating' and artists might even be offended and scared because artificial intelligence can create unique pieces of art that people are excited about.

My mission here is not to judge whether or not you should use these tools. My mission is to let you know this is where the world is moving and you have the opportunity to create things you might not have known how to create before.

I personally see this as an opportunity to challenge what is already in my head. And it empowers authors to do much more of the work in a fun way that speeds up the process and potentially reduces costs significantly.

I suggest you keep an open mind, experiment, and stay focused on how to best get your message across to your readers. Also, the creative mind is still yours. AI tools will create what you ask for. Using AI to create an image is a matter of adding a tool to your toolbox. You still need to be imaginative.

Learn more
visit goosebump.pub/nextgen-author-book

CHAPTER 8

New perception of readers

A diverse set of (overlapping) roles

In chapter 7, I have challenged what a book could look like, how many products can be created from one manuscript, and what a creation process looks like. But before we can conclude on what authorship reimagined looks like we also need to look at the recipient part; the reader.

When you move into the web3 world (which we all will eventually), everything changes in terms of defining the needs and wants of your reader.

It's too simple to use the common categories of *entertain, educate, inspire,* or even *convert* (which should always be at the back of your mind when creating books). In an NFT world, these are no longer the only reasons people buy books.

They might also look for the opportunity to engage in one of these roles:

1. They want to learn about NFTs and get familiar with new technologies;
2. They might be NFT enthusiasts and want to be a part of the development happening in the associated communities;

3. They hope to make an excellent investment and expect to make profit reselling the NFT later at a profit;
4. They might want to be connected with other fans concerned with the same topic you teach;
5. They might want to speculate on flipping rare editions of books;
6. They might be superfans and collect everything you create or everything created in the space you operate;
7. They might want the additional content unlocked with the NFT - or to get access to the events you host, or to other perks like special treatment in your customer service.

Engaged readership

I mentioned some of the above-mentioned scenarios before but I want to direct your attention to how your relationship with your audience can change. The culture among NFT holders is very vibrant and engaging. Humans want to create, be generous and contribute. It's our nature.

Because you can drop new content or add additional utilities to NFT holders, you can much more easily invite readers into the creation process - as opposed to the print regime in which you need to complete the product before launching and in which the product comes as just one piece of content and with no additional utilities - or any connection to the audience. In an NFT world, readers can become your source of inspiration, co-creators of content or even investors in your business.

You can create digital art that features the characters in your book and allow NFT holders to licence them and use them in their own content. Or you can use the metadata from the NFT to give special privileges to those who held onto their NFTs instead of reselling them or those who engaged the most in your community.

At an overall level, you'll need to decide if you want to use your NFT project to:

a. Tap into new segments that are NFT enthusiasts
b. Engage your readers in content creation
c. Engage your readers in a common mission to create a particular change in the world
d. Or to become loyal book fans that will not only buy your next book but become advocates for them and your community

Some of the ways to use NFTs to do the latter include allowing fans to earn book tokens based on ebook reading time or hiding social tokens in your book so readers can go scavenger hunting in your content. I am certain there will be lots of examples of how to use gamification to engage your readers that will also soon be easier to implement.

The possibilities are endless for what you can do with an NFT. Not all are equally accessible at this point, but they will be and you can certainly be creative as is and redefine what the author-reader relationship should be like in your business.

In web2, you have zero information about your readers and it's a lot more complicated to reach them after the initial purchase. All of this changes with web3 and you should map out a vision for how you would like your readers to be a part of your business in the future.

CHAPTER 9
Invested participation

We are slowly but surely moving from Organisation to Organism, and this trend is very much in line with the 'Power to the people' and decentralisation trends. Again, this is not a recent phenomenon. During the 90s and 00s, several researchers and authors described how organisations would benefit from being 'managementless', meaning there would be no hierarchy but teams would self-form and self-manage around projects that people find meaningful.

In hierarchies, we built silos that are dividing people rather than uniting them to solve problems. We built layers through which information is filtered and decisions are delayed. The idea is that these fixed structures will create accountability and that we therefore can control the outcome. There are many problems in that, the biggest one perhaps being that the desired 'outcome' is defined by very few people who are not in sync with either the market or the people who are supposed to produce the outcome.

If you think about it, very few people in this world make most decisions - and more people now realise that decision-makers are not successful in solving the world's major problems. This is feeding the 'power to the people' movement. We need a more planetary view on how to solve problems and we need to work together and across organisational boundaries.

Morning Star is a California-based tomato processing company that adopted self-management in 1990. There is no hierarchy, no bosses, no titles. Each colleague enters the company with the same set of rights as any other colleague. Not a single colleague can force another colleague to do something they don't want to do.

The organisation operates with two key principles: All interactions should be voluntary and you must honour your commitments. Today, Morning Star operates three factories with the largest production scale in the world. Without management. And Morning Star is just one example. The municipality where I live was named Best Public Sector Workplace in Europe after becoming almost management-free (just a few managers acting as facilitators)[60].

These are examples of what's happening within organisations. Researchers within innovation have for decades recommended looser structures and also a much higher degree of openness to the world outside the organisation, like working directly with customers and engaging in collaborative innovation efforts with competitors, to become con-colleagues and co-bake a bigger cake and solve important problems in the world.

We know poor leadership and lack of meaning is the number one reason people leave their job. Significant parts of younger generations, especially the well-educated ones, don't want to be tied up in a job with a manager who tells them how to think or what they should want to become. They prefer creating their own path and select themselves which projects they want to commit to. Like at the Morning Star tomato plant.

* * *

So why am I telling you all this in a book about publishing in a web3 world? Because I want you to be aware of the change happening in how people feel about intermediaries hindering meaningful change from happening and setting rules they have to comply with, whether or not they make sense. This is what's fuelling the decentralisation trend and the power to the people trend, and they are the actual forces behind web3 penetration.

It's a fallacy that we can keep people in line and make them do what they are told. A lot of research has shown that most business strategies are never implemented. They are hot topics of conversation, nothing more. And when people only get a piece of the information, they make sense of it the best they can and add their own beliefs and desires into the mix. This means hardly anyone in a hierarchical organisation has the same idea of what the vision or strategy means, and they end up doing whatever they feel makes more sense.

* * *

Instead of trying to organise for people, we could benefit from accepting we are all part of a living organism with unique parts that interact with each other in whatever way makes the most sense to us, about matters that are important to us.

There is potential in being the facilitator who empowers people to take part in creating change and support import-ant work. People long to belong and to be part of something meaningful; in many cases, people are even willing to pay to participate or invest their time, energy and money in projects they believe in.

Many of the most successful NFT projects offer NFT holders access to a community, either on Telegram or Discord which honestly feels like something from the 90s and has a terrible user interface and can feel very overwhelming and confusing. It has become popular because of its tokengate. You need to verify with your wallet that you hold the NFT that gives access to that part of Discord.

As an author, you can use Discord to give an opportunity to connect in a way that was not there before. Since NFT ownership is required to access your community, you know who in your audience are the most invested people. Because they purchased an NFT/NFT book from you, or because they made an effort to connect with the NFT you give them as a gift.

People can enter the Discord, but that's not in itself going to create much change. You need to focus on empowering the community to become self-led and facilitate that they connect and unite to build a culture and come together to make the community something of real value to its participants. And if you take it up a notch, you consider giving them real (monetary) ownership of the increased value, using a DAO.

* * *

The DAOs make it possible for people to invest, participate in decision making and help create change while increasing the value of their investment at the same time. I briefly explained DAOs in chapter 3, but I'll assume the concept is new to you and you can use a refreshment and that we go a little deeper here:

"A decentralised autonomous organisation (DAO) is an emerging form of legal structure. With no central governing body, every member within a DAO typically shares a common goal and attempts to act in the best interest of the entity."[61]

a.   Authority is distributed among all participants; the collective group of leaders and participants act as the governing body

b.   Individuals can feel more empowered and connected to the entity when they have a direct say and voting power on all matters

c.   Within a DAO, votes are cast via blockchain and made publicly viewable. This incentivises actions that will benefit voters' reputation.

* * *

I am not saying a DAO is the right thing for you. I would need to know a lot more before making such a recommendation. But I encourage you to raise the bar and imagine your *business story* ten years from now:

a.   What change did you create in the world? What is your legacy?

b.   What is the narrative that has connected people to create a better world and/or a better quality of life for a significant number of people?

And when you have clarity on the impact you would like to have, ask yourself:

c. Do you have to do this in a hierarchical form with you as the authority and people as followers?
d. Could you go a step further and not just build a community *for* the participants but build it *with* them?
e. Could you give them real *ownership* and encourage people to go from being involved to being invested? (hint: also a way to raise capital for growth)
f. Could you share your book's success with your audience and create a monetary incentive for them to help you reach more people with your message?
g. Could your role be to form the narrative that will shape imagination and make people believe they can do amazing things - and then offer an arena for them to do that?

* * *

I believe that what web3 can do for authors is to bring authorship and readership closer. It can transform authorship from 'creators of books' to 'creators of conversations' - and it can transform readership from 'consumers of content' into 'creators of change'. All change happening in the world is reflected in our language, and the words we use challenge the mind, shape imagination and facilitate change happening.

This is why I believe creative and visionary authors (and artists in general) are cornerstones in solving bigger world problems. I am aware it may seem far-fetched but the Creator

Economy is here and I am confident that as we adopt and adapt to new business models using web3 technology, the power to create change will belong to creators with the most meaningful narrative and who create a movement around it.

* * *

None of us knows how this will play out in the coming years. But it will play out, I am certain about that. If you think ten years ahead from now, I think you'll agree there is very little chance that things (technology, marketing, business) will remain the same. At some point, you will look back and tell the story about your personal and professional journey in this landscape.

We know organisational structures don't work, aren't respected and that we are all part of one big organism. After reading this book, I hope you know significant change is coming. What I suggest you do as a minimum is:

a. Start *educating yourself* about NFTs, create your wallet and buy just one NFT to get familiar with the concept and process;

b. Revisit your *business narrative* and get clarity on the change you want to make (your impact and legacy);

c. Use your wildest imagination (and then 10x that) and *describe how big this could be* if the right people were involved.

Then (soon) also consider, if you should get an NFT into your reader's wallet (and educate your users on how to create such a wallet). The one undeniable asset in all of this is the value of holding the wallet addresses of people who share your vision.

Every time they log in (whether that's now or something that happens down the road), you will be there. They will see your NFT in there. And if they decide to sell it, you'll get paid whatever royalty is defined in the smart contract for that sale - and you'll then be in someone else's wallet.

The connection between you and the holders of your NFTs is eternal. It's minted on the blockchain and can never be erased. As opposed to, if I buy your course and never revisit it, an NFT is a real asset for you as well as for the NFT holder. You can then later decide if you want to connect the NFT later on to a DAO and give people voting power and ownership to the change you create in conjunction.

Mark Manson (collection)

*The Subtle Art of Not Giving a F*uck* is the first New York Times Bestselling Book to be turned into NFTs.

Author Mark Manson pulled 1,111 unique quotes from the book and used them as the centrepieces of digital art images, which were then published as NFTs. Each art piece contains visual elements that are more or less rare for the collection, making some pieces more valuable than others.

This strategy also gives people interested in the project reason to buy multiple art pieces or (not to be underestimated) spend time discovering which ones are the most interesting ones. Since he uses quotes from the book, there might also be some pieces that resonate more with the buyer's own opinion or what they want to display in the digital wallet.

The NFTs provide the ability to redeem specific rewards, including access to an unreleased chapter, Manson's private web3 society 'Zero Fucks Club' & more. This is the exclusive launchpad community for all of Mark's future web3 projects and an opportunity to connect with the author and other fans in the chat room (all on Discord).

In his FAQ[62], Mark Manson gives reasons for tokenizing his book which include (shortened):

1. I've already seen firsthand the excitement at their (NFTs) potential in the publishing and media industries.
2. NFTs have the potential to solve many of the problems writers face and I want to make ways for authors to enter this space.
3. NFTs allow us to align incentives and value exchange with the true creative process.

The Mark Manson use case is also great for studying and getting inspiration from the full details on what NFT ownership can mean. You can find the link to the Collection FAQ in the endnotes[63].

You can also find a great example of what a webpage for such project might look like and what an NFT roadmap might look like[64]. The existence of a roadmap shows that investing in an NFT is just the start of a journey together with the creator and other NFT holders.

USE CASE
Gary Vee (Book Games)

Gary Vaynerchuk, AKA Gary Vee, is a multi-entrepreneur and four-time New York Times bestselling author, regarded as one of the most important figures in NFTs. Apart from being an NFT collector and creator of the extremely successful VeeFriends, he also launched Vayner3[65] to assist celebrities and brands with their own NFT endeavours.

The VeeFriends series and related so called mini-drops have together generated hundreds of millions of dollars in NFT sales. Holders of the inaugural series 1 NFTs have free access to VeeCon, an annual event with very cool speakers, as well as other perks like meeting up with Gary at his wine store. They also get access to the VeeFriends community, in which Gary is very active.

In August 2021, Book Games was announced as Gary announced his book '*Twelve and a Half: Leveraging the Emotional Ingredients Necessary for Business Success.*'

Book Games included 125,000 burnable tokens (meaning they are 'used up' when you use them) in a game incentivising Vaynerchuk's NFT fan base to purchase as many copies of his new book as they possibly could, to receive NFT rewards down the line.

For every 12 books someone ordered, they would receive one NFT via airdrop. After Gary Vee had sold over *one million copies*, he announced the gamified part of Book Games to go live on January 10, 2022. Now, there is a way to get on the bestseller list!

Book Games holders can sell their NFTs or trade them for other NFTs, sports cards, VeeCon tickets, and other special prizes. Book Games can also act as whitelist access (think of it as a pre-approved waitlist) for other VeeFriends projects[66].

At the time of finishing this book, the least expensive VeeFriends NFT was 5,89 ETH (~$9,375) which excludes many devoted fans from the community.

Vaynerchuk announced to release 55,555 additional NFTs, VeeFriends Series 2, priced at $995 USD in ETH per token. This NFT will, however, not give VeeCon access. People buy anyway because this is Gary Vee - and they expect cool things happening down the road for them too.

USE CASE
Sitka World (co-writing)

Sitka World's vision is to become "the go-to hub for creative writers in Web3, fully embracing the magic within us while reshaping Web3 through the power of storytelling."[67] They offer participants one or more of three different roles: Book-worm (reader), Scribe (creative writer), or Degen (here for the money).

Readers can be a part of the journey of building a fantasy world, both to contribute ideas and share the project's financial rewards.

At least three books will be published and contributing members of the community will receive 50% all royalties, including those from NFT sales, e-books, physical books, and audiobooks. In short, it's an immersive gamified fantasy ecosystem with shared profits. They also offer workshops, events, and resources to help people improve their writing craft.

An interesting aspect of this project is that the books are published as 3 acts each. The first is purchased as a genesis NFT, the next two are given to holders of the first. When all 3 acts are published, the act-NFTs are burned and turned into a book-NFT.

Get the Goosebump Author NFT

visit goosebump.pub/nft

PART 4
Start The NFT Engines

The future is here.
It's just not evenly distributed

- WILLIAM GIBSON

CHAPTER 10
Emotional triggers

What comes first? The book, the audience, or the NFT? The short answer is, you work with what you've got. The longer answer is, it depends on the value you want the NFT to create. Let's break it down.

Like in any other marketing initiative, you need to know not only who your audience is but know what they want and need - and which emotional response you need to trigger.

Some products in themselves trigger specific emotional responses (like private jets) but for other products, it all comes down to how you package and communicate them. Like milk which is no longer just one kind but many stories people tell about themselves when making their choice. To identify how you can package and communicate an NFT project to *your* audience, you need to consider what makes them tick.

The segmentation model 'Emotional Customer Types', which is based on phd-research[68], outlines four response patterns[69]. We all have multiple or all of these patterns but typically one is dominant. You can use the emotional customer types to figure out what an NFT project might look like for you.

A person with a predominantly **blue** profile prefers to engage with high-quality, high-end brands. This person makes 'safe' purchases and invests in areas with proven results so they are not likely to invest in a volatile, unfamiliar market. They are not first movers but, on the other hand, they seek to be modern and knowledgeable about technology and finance.

The blue person will invest in prestigious NFT projects to be an interesting person in conversations, or in crypto when people in his/her circle believe it's a better deal than stocks. They want a high service level and only have to learn the least amount of new stuff as possible. They prefer just placing an order. If they need teaching, they will seek out the most prominent in the market to teach them.

A person with a **green** profile seeks security, stability and predictability. They are not likely to be first-movers and they will always prefer what they already know. Once they realise that NFTs are here to stay, you will be their hero if you provide simple and very clear instructions on what they need to do. Simple does not mean high-level but detailed and easy to follow step-by-step.

If you have a green following today, focus on getting as many of them onboard as possible and ensure you get testimonials from them. A green person's second choice after doing what they usually do, is to do what others are generally recommending. You will need to be very clear on what the NFT can do and explain the process of saying yes and getting onboard. A comparison chart showing what is similar (or merits) and what is different (or demerits) in purchasing your hardcover and your NFT version will help them decide.

A person with a dominant **yellow** doesn't need all the details beforehand. If they are already in your engaged community, they might be onboard because it's something the group can conquer together. They will feel special if your NFT is only for the group or if they can invite a friend. Yellow people seek to be taken care of and to take care of others. Your NFT project should not only look 'cozy' but pristine and be related to building a community. Even better if it helps them help others.

People who are predominantly **red** don't look for risk-free projects because they love everything new and different. They want stimuli that will kill boredom. The last thing they want is stability and predictability. They want excitement and to be challenged. They are always looking for the next level of weirdness, meaningfulness, and opportunity to grow. If you have a red audience, they will be excited that you talk about something that forces them to look up things and learn unfamiliar words.

So...

Step #1 is to identify *what is the dominant emotional response pattern in your audience* which you can think of as: "What is the story my audience typically tells themselves when making purchases or committing to something new?"

Who is the most similar to yours?
- ☐ "I am a rational person and choose this because it's the best product/expert with proven results for people like me." - **Blue**
- ☐ "I choose what I know works and what most people say delivers value for money." - **Green**
- ☐ "I choose this because I like the personality of the teacher and there is a great community where people help each other." - **Yellow**
- ☐ "I am different and innovative and this is exciting. I am in!" - **Red**

Step #2 is to get clarity of the *design criteria* for your NFT project. What will interest them and what will be turn-off?

If **blue**, your strategy should focus on presenting your NFT as:
- ☐ An investment that is likely to be profitable
- ☐ Knowledge that is career enhancing
- ☐ Something other people in their industry or recognised people in publishing are concerned with (take the weirdness out of it)
- ☐ A beautiful, new but classic product in beautiful, clean wrapping

If **green**, your strategy should focus on presenting your NFT as:
- ☐ Not as different as they think; with advantages explained in clear language
- ☐ Something they can try risk-free with easy-to-follow instructions, a solid FAQ and a guarantee you will help them if they have any problems buying, using, or selling it

If **yellow**, your strategy should focus on presenting your NFT as:
- ☐ Their key tool to be a part of building the community
- ☐ A fun challenge to which they can invite others
- ☐ Something that can make their everyday life better in a fun or rewarding way

If **red**, your strategy should focus on presenting your NFT as:

- ☐ The next big thing nobody knows about
- ☐ Something they can get exclusive access to (if they can solve the puzzle)
- ☐ Something they can use to create projects of their own
- ☐ Something all the really cool people do, and only them

With that, you can move on to defining your NFT project.

CHAPTER 11

What they will pay for

Back to the question from the previous chapter: Should you start with the audience, the book or the NFT? Before answering that question, let's just quickly refresh why people buy so we can align your campaign with your goals.

People might buy your NFTs for one, several or many of these reasons:

- ☐ They appreciate the design or artistry of the piece. They have a *collectors* mindset;
- ☐ They are *superfans* of and collect many different (all!) items available from your brand;
- ☐ They want to show their *support* and appreciation for all you do for them, and may not have any intention to use or resell it;
- ☐ They want to be part of the *mission* you are on and help solve an important problem in the world;
- ☐ They see the NFT as an *investment*, betting that the value of the NFT will increase over time so they can resell at a higher price;
- ☐ They are vivid *readers* and want to purchase more books (reselling digital books)
- ☐ They want to *learn about NFTs* and you happen to be one they trust who introduced it first;
- ☐ They want to *crowdfund* and pre-order/validate the market - because they want the book;
- ☐ They want the *merchandise* you offer with your NFT;
- ☐ They want to own a limited, special or unique *edition* of the book;
- ☐ They want to belong to the smaller part that are the *inner circle* of your bigger community;
- ☐ They want *licensing* rights to one of the characters in your book
- ☐ They want to know they can *safely buy* books in secondary markets to save money or too not contribute to overproduction without violating copyrights and compensating the creator;
- ☐ They want to be part of a new *trend*;

- [ ] They want *voting* rights in the community or DAO;
- [ ] They need the NFT to access your exciting *events* in the metaverse
- [ ] They want access to elevated *service* level;
- [ ] They want a *tokengate* to log in to your membership with their digital wallet so they don't need another password;
- [ ] They prefer that the *creator* receives most of the royalties;
- [ ] They are willing to pay a higher price because they expect you to *airdrop* more value later to the NFT;
- [ ] They want the NFT version because you made that version more *interactive* and interesting;
- [ ] They want to get the *complimentary items* you included in the NFT apart from the book;
- [ ] They want to *give away* the book to someone in a fun way and help them learn about NFTs;
- [ ] They want to support that you, as the creator, get *paid now* and not in months;
- [ ] They want to get involved in the project and *help* it become successful as a testament to their love for the brand;
- [ ] They want access to engage in fun ways with *other superfans.*

There is no limit to how long this list could be. If you come up with great ideas, please share them at goosebump.world (you'll get a free membership).

CHAPTER 12
Your goals

Getting early into NFTs might not seem a necessity to you, and it probably isn't. It is indeed an *opportunity* though! So instead of explaining why you can't live without it, I am encouraging you to *first* consider what could be your reasons to go all in, *then* consider your reasons to choose being a follower instead of a leader.

OK, now I have to start with the latter, don't you think? Because choosing your role in the world must be the starting point of your business strategy.

In his book 'Tribes: We need you to lead us', Seth Godin (acknowledged marketing genius) says: "True leaders have figured out that the real win is in turning a casual fan into a true one"..."What they demand, though, is generosity and bravery".

Whatever the status quo is, changing it makes you remarkable. To make people follow you, take a cause that's worth fighting for.

Knowing my authors, I know they all started their business to not have a dictating boss but be their own, to use their full potential, and to have freedom to choose what they work for, who they work for, when they work and where they work. But they are also almost always passionate about their subject because they found a better way to solve an important problem.

We need more leaders. We need the bravery to pursue the bigger mission. And to succeed in that, we need to be more appreciative of people who want to join us on that journey. As Godin says: "The easiest thing is to react. The second easiest thing is to respond. The hardest thing is to initiate". I might add: "The only way not to get bored in your own business is to purposely initiate transformational change". Entrepreneurs are builders. We accept risk. And we create landmarks that didn't exist before. You can't lead without imagination.

Since you have read so far, I'll assume you are or want to be a leader. The good news is, says Godin, that you are only one small step away from being one. You just need to *decide* you are a leader.

* * *

When I took a 10-week road trip from Denmark to Spain and all the way around the Iberic Island last year, I was listening to Simon Sinek's book 'Find your why'. Not 'Start with why', which is another book, but 'Find your why'.

It suggests you start with the question: "Why do I want a business?". Think about it long enough to respond in 1-2 sentences.

Then ask: "Why?" again. And again. And again. Seven times, you ask Why. This will bring you to the real reason, often through a quite painful realisation about the significance and presence of something that happened in the past.

I know, this might seem a little off topic, but this is something I encourage my authors to do. When you know *why* you want your business, you will also know your *mission*, *who* you want to attract, and *how* you want them involved in your mission and business:

a. Do you want to offer them ownership, voting rights, licensing rights?
b. Do you want them to be interested, involved or invested in your business?
c. Is your book a one-off product or do you want creating books to be a much more significant part of your business activity?
d. Do you need a way to more clearly differentiate your business from the competition?
e. Do you want to reach bigger audiences, using your NFT project to create awareness?
f. Do you want to create a true legacy?
g. Do you want to stretch your imagination of what's possible?

Did I hear you say "yes, yes, and yes" but also a "but"? I am guessing the two most common reasons for deciding to wait until the proofs of these being successful strategies are visible in your very near neighbourhood are 1) doubt if your audience is ready, and 2) if you are ready.

To that, I want to be frank with you. If you are not a leader, you are a follower. But you *will* have to deal with this. Web3 is happening and your audience is already moving too. They will create their digital wallet in a minute. They will log in to their favourite Facebook group with the NFT they hold in their wallet in a minute. Nine months ago, I knew nothing about this topic. Now I see NFTs everywhere. It is only a matter of paying attention and leaning into it. Then you will be able to make this your next thing!

CHAPTER 13
Is it time?

"Malene, the concept looks great but you forget that our customers will never use SMS". That was the response I received from a C-level manager in the company I worked for when presenting a mobile solution for customers to purchase insurance and report damages back in 2008.

That's 15 years ago. It's when everybody also said Facebook was for tecnagers (now it's for grandparents). Since then, everybody moved from text, to images, to video and full on mobile. People are not spectators anymore but creators of the internet. If you think about how fast you went from wired phone lines, phone books and tangible photo albums to an everyday life in which digital is an integral part of everyone's lives, there is no way there is not a next big thing after video and smartphones.

Global eSport fandom is expected to reach 532 million people, with half being enthusiasts and half being occasional viewers[70]. This is 20% more than the entire population of South America and very close to the entire Spanish-speaking population in the world, bearing witness to the fact that a large group of people speaks 'eSport' now. Global eSports revenue was valued at $1.08 billion in 2021 and it's forecast to grow to 1.62 billion in 2024[71]. I didn't know eSport was such a big thing until I started writing this book. But that does not mean it's not real, does it?

Did you know gamers make up more than a third of the world population?[72] And it's not just dorky teenage boys who are gaming. The average age of gamers is 34 years[73]. An average gamer owns a house and has child(ren)! A quarter of gamers are between 34 and 54 years old. And in the US, 45% of gamers are female[74]. It's a thriving industry attracting all kinds of people. One of the Augmented Reality games most widely known is 'Pokemon Go'. Though it's a free game, it reached a 6 billion USD revenue by 2020 and was downloaded 572 million times in 2021[75]. You might have been one of the people who were scavenger hunting for Pokemons a few years back.

What is my point?

These segments are not distinct groups of people who differ from others. They are just *early adopters* (or majority adopters) and open to new ways of connecting and engaging with each other, creating and exploring digital worlds and monetizing new technologies. You might be a later adopter but you might also not have been the first to adopt the smartphone. I bet you can't imagine the world without it now.

Someone was the person you trusted who introduced you to mobile technology. It was awkward at first but then it got easier. Now that you know more about web3 than most, you have a chance to get ahead and capture attention in your niche and be the one to teach them. Like I said, I knew nothing about this nine months ago and I am pretty sure you learned a lot in this book, even if not all and the learning curve felt steep. You will soon realise it's not too complicated.

It is time. If not today, very, very soon.

Learn how you can write a great book faster
and use fun and unsual marketing strategies to sell it.

Create your Goosebump Free login at:
goosebump.pub

Vocabulary for noobs

Airdrop or drop Harry Potter's owl that brings only good news. More value to the NFT holder. Good way to keep your NFT holders happy. Some owls are shitty owls (scam) so do open one from an unknown sender.

Creator token A currency in which to earn and spend inside the realm of a specific community. Also known as creator coins or social token.

Crypto coin The same as cryptocurrencies or digital cash. I am sure you heard of Bitcoin. Ether is also popular. There are many different coins.

Crypto exchange A crypto exchange is a website on which you can buy and sell digital money to put in your wallet.

Cryptocurrencies See Crypto coin.

Gas fees   Yeah, the nerds want somehow to get paid for their trouble, depending on how busy they are when you want to make a transfer, a fee will be calculated for you. You could get up at 2am to make the transfer and get a better price. No one else wants to, so the nerds are less busy. It's really a supply and demand situation going on.

Marketplace   Where you buy and sell NFTs. Go play at Opensea.io (no financial advice implied).

Minting   When a bunch of computer nerds makes sure your transactions are set in stone, a.k.a., recorded on the blockchain.

NFT   Someone must get off by introducing a word nobody knows. You are cool now, because you know NFT stands for Non-*Fungible* Token - and that non-fungible means that each NFT is unique. A dollar bill or social token is not unique. There are many that are similar, so they are fungible. But there are no two same NFTs. Even if they are represented by the same digital image. The most interesting part about an NFT is *utility* (what it can do).

NFT collection   A bunch of pretty or ugly pictures that people fuss about because they are cool to own. They are interesting if your audience has a collectors mindset. If not, add some *utility* (what the NFT can do). If you publish a series of NFTs they will together be called a collection.

Social token   See Creator token.

Unlockable   Do something, get something. Unlockable content is content that is only available if the NFT gives access to it.

Wallet   Imagine you went to the supermarket. You paid with something from your wallet and put the carrots you buy back into the wallet. It's kind of like that. When you want access to my 'Rabbits Only Club', you show me you have a carrot in your wallet. All transactions happen with a wallet. You need one (or more). It could be MetaMask. You also need to put some cryptomoney in it (sometimes you can pay with FIAT which is just a weird word for dollars, euro and other non-crypto currencies.)

Did you love this book?

Please give it a review on Amazon.

This will help me get it on front of more people.

Then send me a screenshot of your review to
mb@malenebendtsen.com
to receive a small token of my appreciation.

Acknowledgements
and the story of NextGen Author

I'm a huge fan of Social Media Examiner. At the end 2021, I heard Michael Stelzner talk about his interest for crypto and NFTs and I quickly realised that what I had worked with as a wild innovative idea back in 2009 (Second Life and Bitcoin), was now surfacing and becoming something to pay attention to.

I started listening to podcasts and by January 2022, I was convinced web3 would become a significant topic at the Social Media Marketing World, a San Diego conference by Social Media Examiner that I am a devoted fan of. If you follow me, you know I so much *loooove* that conference!

I had made this year's visit, a month-long visit in the US, meeting with partners and crossing the entire country by train and car. Hey! Nobody ever sees what it's in the middle and I was wondering!

Before I arrived in San Diego, I created my digital wallet and educated myself on the basics. And like I expected, crypto was *the* topic of the year and we all received an NFT at the end of the conference.

Meanwhile, I was doing research. You see all of the speakers are also very successful authors and I asked them about how they saw web3 being relevant to authors. Everyone agreed their books are their most valuable assets, and NFTs are for assets, ... but nobody had thought it through yet. This was in

March 2022, and I stuck with my strategy of interviewing successful authors for my new podcast.

So I made a lot of interviews in the following months, while also immersing myself into the web3 world. A few things happened over the summer that made me leave the intended new podcast behind and decide to dig deeper into web3 instead. One of them was that I began seeing web3/book-related hashtags showing up on internet and conversations. I saw many of the big fashion brands go into NFTs. I saw a significant book distributor start an NFT project (which I invested in).

By the time, my peers went on summer vacations, I blocked out everything apart from my daughter's wedding to lay out a strategy for a new book, a new platform for progressive authors and for my NFT strategy.

I built it all in just under a month and then invited my audience to get behind the scenes to see me write this book. I shared everything I learnt in the process with them. I also showed them exactly what I did. Why? So I could get their feedback and questions while building the content and thinking through my recommendations.

In 30 days throughout August, I created this book with the help of my new friend Jasper. After spending the first ten days, making a solid plan and making all decisions about the content based on research, Jasper and I quickly put together a rough draft which I could then improve. I then had a few beta readers apart from the content I shared on the fly. From there, I used another AI tool to improve the text, and yet another one to create the illustration for the cover. Finally, I sent it all to a line editor and proofreader to correct my non-native English and remove all my mistakes. From start to finish in 45 days - and I am so damn proud of what this book ended up being!

Why am I telling you this story? Because I want to say that writing and publishing a book is easy if you have something important to say. Raise the bar for the change you want to make, dedicate full time for a short period and you'll quickly be ready to claim your spot in the world. This book is my claim to NextGen Authorship ;)

My audience and authors have given me valuable feedback and questions I couldn't answer yet. Thank you for that! You are my inspiration and you all do amazing things in your businesses!

Jesper Bram, Anders Tilsted, Carolyn Harder, Iben Posniak, Susanne Aalborg, Liam Naden, and Sanne Dollerup were my daily supporters who challenged me to go deeper, raise the bar, and helped me by checking for accuracy. They were also my cheerleaders when I was almost puking from exhaustion or pulling my hair out in frustration. Oh, what a nice little message with encouragement can do to keep your head straight ;)

Thank you to everyone who was a part of this journey. You all know who you are in my life. You mean the world to me and this book is in your honour.

About the author

Malene is the former CEO of a self publishing company, covering Latin America. She is also a former director of innovation, specialised in industry disruption and business model innovation.

She is an author and a business strategist teaching experts, teachers, public speakers and other freedom seekers how to write, publish and market their books. She is also the editor of more than 30 nonfiction books, which on average, sold 5x market average and created significant business growth for the author.

Malene is a futurist at heart and as a business model innovator, she is determined to find new ways for authors to connect with their audience and strategically use their books to build their businesses. As a publishing rebel and a knowledge liberator, there are no darlings she won't kill.

 Goosebump is a membership for progressive authors and creative minds. *For more information, visit goosebump.pub.*

 Connect with Malene and Goosebump on LinkedIn, Twitter, or have fun with us on TikTok.

Endnotes

1   Berkeley Liberation program, 1969
2   https://en.wikipedia.org/wiki/David_Chaum
3   Accenture, https://www.raconteur.net/the-future-of-blockchain-in-8-charts/
4   https://cwbsa.com/innovation-adoption-curve
5   https://www.forbes.com/sites/michaeldelcastillo/2019/04/16/blockchain-50-billion-dollar-babies
6   https://www.forbes.com/sites/abrambrown/2021/12/01/crypto-tokens-people-constitution-dao-ether-redeem-refund/
7   https://www.cnbc.com/2021/11/16/dao-raises-millions-in-eth-to-bid-on-copy-of-us-constitution.html
8   https://www.theverge.com/22820563/constitution-meme-47-million-crypto-crowdfunding-blockchain-ethereum-constitution.
9   https://bitcoinist.com/constitution-dao-lost-auction-to-41m-bid-but-made-history-what-happens-now/
10   https://podcasts.apple.com/dk/podcast/crypto-business/id1602744952?i=1000552914212
11   https://www.constitutiondao.com/
12   https://www.statista.com/markets/417/topic/477/books-publishing/#overview
13   https://www.statista.com/statistics/271931/revenue-of-the-us-book-publishing-industry/
14   https://www.publishersweekly.com/pw/by-topic/industry-news/publisher-news/article/89038-over-the-past-25-years-the-big-publishers-got-bigger-and-fewer.html
15   https://www.bookbusinessmag.com/post/big-5-financial-reports-reveal-state-traditional-book-publishing/
16   https://mybookcave.com/authorpost/what-are-the-big-5-publishers/
17   https://us.macmillan.com/publishers/
18   https://www.kirkusreviews.com/news-and-features/articles/the-big-five-become-the-big-four/
19   https://www.authorsalliance.org/2022/07/29/update-antitrust-and-the-proposed-penguin-random-house-and-simon-schuster-merger/

20 https://www.publishersweekly.com/pw/by-topic/indus-try-news/publisher-news/article/88925-america-s-biggest-pub-lishers-keep-posting-a-profit.html

21 https://www.statista.com/statistics/184390/number-of-estab-lishments-in-us-publishing-industries-since-2001

22 https://blog.bizvibe.com/blog/top-book-publishing-companies

23 https://www.investopedia.com/terms/i/industrylifecycle.asp

24 https://www.investopedia.com/terms/i/industrylifecycle.asp

25 https://www.bookbusinessmag.com/post/big-5-financial-re-ports-reveal-state-traditional-book-publishing/

26 https://www.tagari.com/how-many-books-are-published-in-the-world/ and https://www.tonerbuzz.com/blog/how-many-books-are-published-each-year/

27 https://www.blueoceanstrategy.com/what-is-blue-ocean-strate-gy/

28 http://ibm.com

29 https://explodingtopics.com/blog/number-of-cryptocurrencies

30 https://www.youtube.com/watch?v=97ufCT6lQcY&ab_chan-nel=TEDxTalks

31 https://www.zippia.com/advice/how-many-businesses-ac-cept-bitcoin

32 https://www.zippia.com/advice/how-many-businesses-ac-cept-bitcoin

33 https://cointelegraph.com/news/99-98-less-power-lighthouse-s-first-ethereum-and-eth2-merge-transaction

34 https://maketafi.com/coca-cola-nft

35 https://global.nissannews.com/en/releases/nissan-unveils-all-new-ev-in-the-metaverse

36 https://metaversefashionweek.com/

37 https://www.youtube.com/watch?v=iwyyxEJCIuU&ab_chan-nel=GaryVee

38 https://www.youtube.com/watch?v=B3Ml5y8pDjs&t=0s

39 https://podcasts.apple.com/dk/podcast/crypto-business/id1602744952?i=1000553698212

40 https://www.business2community.com/nft-news/visa-creator-program-for-nfts-commerce-02462930

41 https://www.business2community.com/nft-news/visa-creator-program-for-nfts-commerce-02462930

42 https://queue-it.com/blog/nfts-for-retailers/

43 https://stories.starbucks.com/press/2022/starbucks-brewing-revolutionary-web3-experience-for-its-starbucks-rewards-members/

44 https://www.shopify.com/tokengated-commerce

45 https://twitter.com/RoyalMintUK

46 https://www.business2community.com/nft-news/uk-regulate-stablecoins-crypto-hub-02464468

47 https://www.business2community.com/nft-news/amazon-nft-marketplace-possible-02468908

48 https://business.ticketmaster.com/business-solutions/nfl-partners-with-ticketmaster-to-offer-limited-edition-nfts-to-celebrate-super-bowl-lvi

49 https://www.cryptotechwomennft.com/

50 https://medium.com/geekculture/a-beginners-guide-to-understanding-pfp-nfts-8714e9d30d0b

51 https://www.loeb.com/en/insights/publications/2022/04/brands-and-nfts-licensing-and-contracting-considerations

52 https://www.loeb.com/en/insights/publications/2022/04/brands-and-nfts-licensing-and-contracting-considerations

53 https://boredapeyachtclub.com/#/terms

54 https://en.wikipedia.org/wiki/Big3

55 https://www.sportspromedia.com/news/big3-basketball-nfts-ownership-ice-cube/ *and* https://big3.com/news/everything-you-need-to-know-about-big3-ownership-nfts-minting-may-8th/

56 https://www.neverfeartruth.com/

57 https://www.oldest.org/culture/books-ever-existed/

58 https://en.wikipedia.org/wiki/IBM_Watson

59 https://www.jasper.ai/art

60 https://f5.dk/lederudvikling-selvledelse-er-kun-interessant-hvis-det-skaber-resultater/

61 https://www.investopedia.com/tech/what-dao/

62 https://www.bookcoin.com/subtle-art

63 https://help.bookcoin.com/Collection-FAQs/keFW6X286EYG-31Su72oWQt

64 https://www.bookcoin.com/subtle-art

65 https://vaynernft.co/

66 https://nftnow.com/guides/ultimate-guide-to-veefriends/

67 https://www.sitkaworld.com/home-scribe

68 https://vbn.aau.dk/da/publications/engaging-the-shopping-experience-experience-design-as-a-way-to-in

69 A further development based on: Panksepp, J. (1998). Affective Neuroscience. The Foundations of Human and Animal Emotions. Oxford: Oxford University Press

70 https://newzoo.com/insights/articles/the-esports-audience-will-pass-half-a-billion-in-2022-as-revenue-engagement-esport-industry-growth

71 https://www.statista.com/statistics/490522/global-esports-market-revenue/

72 https://www.insiderintelligence.com/content/gamers-make-up-more-than-one-third-of-world-population

73 https://techjury.net/blog/video-game-demographics/#gref

74 https://www.statista.com/statistics/232383/gender-split-of-us-computer-and-video-gamers/

75 https://www.businessofapps.com/data/pokemon-go-statistics

Printed in Poland
by Amazon Fulfillment
Poland Sp. z o.o., Wrocław

15534206R00087